In the Middle of the Middle Ages

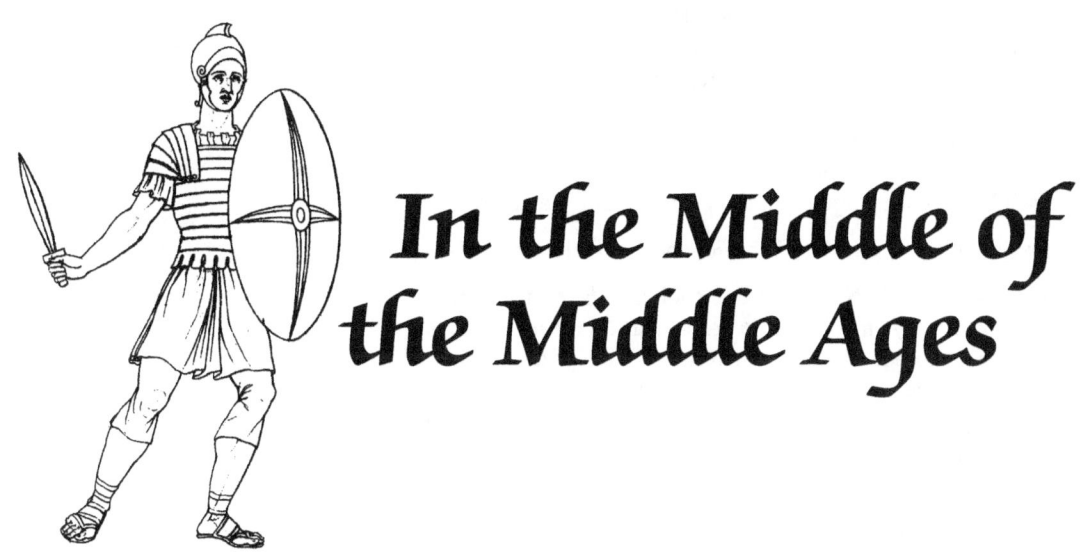

In the Middle of the Middle Ages

Integrating Content Standards and the Arts

Mary Wheeler and Jill Terlep

Music by Mary Wheeler
Illustrations by Jill Terlep

Teacher Ideas Press, an imprint of Libraries Unlimited
Westport, Connecticut • London

Library of Congress Cataloging-in-Publication Data

Wheeler, Mary, 1944-
  In the middle of the Middle Ages : integrating content standards
and the arts / by Mary Wheeler and Jill Terlep.
     p. cm.
  Includes bibliographical references and index.
  ISBN 1-59158-417-5 (pbk : alk. paper)
   1. History—Study and teaching (Elementary)—Activity programs.
  2. Civilization, Medieval—Study and teaching (Elementary)—Activity
programs. 3. Education—Standards—United States.   I. Terlep, Jill.
  II. Title.
  LB1581.W443   2007
  372.5—dc22   2006030914
British Library Cataloguing in Publication Data is available.

Copyright © 2007 by Mary Wheeler and Jill Terlep

All rights reserved. No part of this book may be reproduced
in any form or by any electronic or mechanical means, including
information storage and retrieval systems, without permission in
writing from the publisher, except by a reviewer, who may quote brief
passages in a review. Reproducible pages may be copied for classroom
and educational programs only.

Library of Congress Catalog Card Number: 2006030914
ISBN: 1-59158-417-5

First published in 2007

Libraries Unlimited/Teacher Ideas Press, 88 Post Road West, Westport, CT 06881
A Member of the Greenwood Publishing Group, Inc.
www.lu.com

Printed in the United States of America

The paper used in this book complies with the
Permanent Paper Standard issued by the National
Information Standards Organization (Z39.48–1984).

10 9 8 7 6 5 4 3 2 1

Copyright Acknowledgments

The authors and publisher gratefully acknowledge permission for use of the following material:

National Standards for Arts Education. Copyright © 1994 by Music Educators National Conference (MENC). Used by permission. The complete National Arts Standards and additional materials relating to the Standards are available from MENC – The National Association for Music Education, 1806 Robert Fulton Drive, Reston, VA 20191.

Excerpts from *National Standards s for History, Basic Edition © 1996*, reprinted with permission of the National Center for History in the Schools, UCLA (http://nchs.ucla.edu).

Excerpts from the *Standards Correlation Table for the English Language Arts*. Copyright © 1996 by the International Reading Association and the National Council of Teachers of English. Published by the International Reading Association and the National Council of Teachers of English, reprinted with permission.

Contents

Acknowledgments ix
Introduction xi

Where Do I Start? ... How to Use This Book Effectively 1
   Standards Correlations Introduction 3
   Correlations to National Standards for History K–4 4
   Correlations to National Standards for History 5–12 6
   Correlations to Standards for the English Language Arts 8
   Correlations to the National Standards for Arts Education 10

Teacher Resources 11
Background Information and Rhymes, Guided Activities
   Song and Rhyme Synopsis 12
   Middle Ages Overview 13
      Middle Ages Rhyme 16
      Study Questions 18
   Illuminations
      Setting the Stage, Background Information 20
      Application, Decision Making, Historic Illustration 21
   Traveling Minstrel
      Setting the Stage, Background Information 23
      Factual Recall, Music Composition 24
   Salted Meats and Pickled Beets
      Setting the Stage, Background Information 25
      Compare/Contrast 27
   Marching to the Crusades
      Setting the Stage, Background Information 29
      Multiple Choice 31
   Sun Up, Sun Down (A Peasant's Life)
      Setting the Stage, Background Information 33
      Journal Entry 35
   Sir Richard, Child to Knight
      Setting the Stage, Background Information 36
      Dialogue Writing 38
   Pillory on the Village Green
      Setting the Stage, Background Information 39
      Listing, True/False 41

Castle in Motion
- Setting the Stage, Background Information 42
- Letter Writing 44

This Riddle
- Setting the Stage, Background Information 45
- Factual Recall, Mathematics Reasoning 47

Two Cows
- Setting the Stage, Background Information 49
- Persuasive Writing, Concept Illustration 51

Castle Terms
- Castle Terms Vocabulary 52
- Castle Terms Crossword Puzzle 54
- *Castle in Progress,* Design, Plan 55

Medieval Terms
- Medieval Terms Vocabulary 56
- Medieval Terms Crossword Puzzle 58
- *A Story for the Ages,* Vocabulary Assessment, Creative Writing 59

Medieval Figures
- Medieval Figures Vocabulary 60
- Medieval Figures Crossword Puzzle 62
- *Medieval Figure—A Biography,* Biographical Book Report 63
- *Middle Ages Figures,* Math Assessment 64

Setting the Stage Additional Reading List 65

Research and Discovery Activities 69
- *Who's Who around the Table,* Writing a Narrative 70
- *Books Change History,* Contrast, Ranking 72
- *Perpetual Lamps and Flying Machines,* Scientific Method, Project 73
- *Choose Your Weapons,* Math Calculations, Problem Solving 75
- *Water, Water Everywhere,* Geographical Analysis, Drama Script 76
- *It's Time,* Research, Timeline 77
- *Johann Gutenberg Was the Best Inventor,* Fact or Opinion 78
- *Plague or Famine?,* Research Report 79
- *Tall Cathedrals Touch the Sky,* Identify, Picture, Report 81
- *Black Death! Comparison Table,* Part I, Math Rounding, Table Analysis 83
- *Black Death! Comparison Table,* Part II, Graphing 84
- *A Dragon, Can You Imagine?,* Mythological Illustration 85
- *The Normans Are Coming! Details at Eleven,* Speech 86
- *Read All about It,* Fiction Book Report 87
- *Tournament Adventure,* Creative Writing 89
- *Heraldry, In the Heat of Battle,* Study and Design 90
- *Come to the Fair, Part I,* Plan, List 92
- *Come to the Fair, Part II,* Recall, Listening, Evaluation, Communication 93
- *Come to the Fair, Part III,* Diagram 94
- *Do You Need a Hurdy-Gurdy?,* Research, Presentation 95

    Picture the Past, Graphic Sources 96
    A Pyramid of Power, Critical Thinking 98
    In the Spirit of the Moment, Interview 99
    Gifted and Talented 100
    Cross Curriculum ... More Activities 102
    Answer Key 108
    Answer Key—Crossword Puzzles 110

The Play 112
    Synopsis 113
    Scenes and Musical Sequence Outline 114
    Song Notes 115
    Costumes and Cast of Characters 117
    Props, Backdrop, and Stage Setup 120
    Play Performance Tips 121
    Homeschool Suggestions for the Play 124

The Play: *In the Middle of the Middle Ages* 125
    Teacher Management
    Audition Organization, and Evaluations 184
    Audition Evaluation Forms 185
    Audition Letter to Students, *Lights! Camera! Action!* 186
    Cast (Note Pad) 187
    Songs (Note Pad) 188
    Introductory Letter to Parents 190
    Permission to Videotape 191
    Volunteer Letter to Parents 192
    Letter and Invitation to Staff 193
    Prop Check List 195
    Performance Checklist 196

Bibliography 197
Additional Reading List 199

Acknowledgments

Thank You to

... the children who participated in the production.

... all of the wonderful people who have helped and inspired us through the years.

... Michelle Barnes for always knowing where to find the answer, to everything!

... Janet Compton for ideas and more.

... Jane Kuhn for being a great instructor and teaching architecture and ancient history along with Latin and English.

... the staff in the Nichols Library Children's Reference Department (Naperville, Illinois).

... Charlie Klumpp for unhesitating help, support, expertise, and friendship.

... Elizabeth Budd for embracing our project with enthusiasm and dedication.

Special Acknowledgment and Thank You to

Gary Walters, Butler University; Indianapolis, Indiana;
for the musical arrangements and transcriptions.

and

... Jeff Terlep and John Wheeler for your support, ideas, and faith in us.

This book is for Lauren and Drew.

Mary & Jill

Introduction

From the beginning of children's education, we use simple melodies to help them memorize ABCs and learn to count. Songs and rhymes help people of all ages remember information. This resource book for your instruction about the Middle Ages uses music, literature, and drama, along with other innovative and traditional methods of teaching.

With its very flexible format, this material can be presented in musical form or as rhyming verse. For grades 4 through 8, it can be used by an entire class in a regular setting or in individual learning stations, as extra credit work, or as a gifted and talented project. It is all up to you. See the "Where Do I Start?" section that follows for more ideas.

The play at the end is another rewarding experience for your students. It can be acted in class, read silently, or performed for an audience.

Can you remember asking a parent or friend to "Watch me!" as you danced, sang, or recited information as you were growing up? Even most adults love to entertain audiences. If you choose to stage the play, it is a memory that your students will treasure. Producing a program of this magnitude is a big project, but it is also a fun and satisfying one. It is impossible to forget the faces of the students, friends, and family members during the show.

This book covers many important facets of the Middle Ages, from the systems of feudalism and heraldry to the lives of peasants and knights. When studying the Middle Ages, it is impossible to ignore the importance of religion on people's lives, particularly the impact of the Crusades. Yet although that historic occurrence was Christian, whether the beliefs were Buddhist, Christian, Hindu, Islamic, Judaism, or other, the spiritual convictions directed their followers' lives, along with their social and political decisions.

Speaking to a woman of another faith, one that experienced huge increases in numbers in the Middle Ages, we told her we needed to make certain that our statements were correct. She answered our specific questions, then left the school but returned several minutes later with a book. It was one that explained basic tenets of her faith. As she handed it over for our reference, she said, "We must begin by teaching the children." By that she meant, specifically, teaching them to respect and tolerate the views of others.

Activities in this book encourage children to learn and explore. They are thought-provoking, yet enjoyable. With your help, respectfulness and tolerance are also promoted. When you use this book, you offer an opportunity for children—and adults—to learn the history of the Middle Ages in a unique and unforgettable way.

Illuminations are decorations on the pages of the books of yesterday.
Illuminations—Learn information.
Let us see how others used to work and play.

We'd love to hear from you. Enjoy!

Mary and Jill
maryandjill@teacherstoo.com or www.teacherstoo.com

Where Do I Start?

Our favorite element of the book *In the Middle of the Middle Ages* is its flexibility. What you do is up to you.

From the feudal system that developed after the fall of the Roman Empire to the Crusades and the invention of the printing press by Johann Gutenberg, events and discoveries of the Middle Ages continue to affect our society today.

In the Middle of the Middle Ages is a teacher resource book containing ten original songs/rhymes about topics that shaped the history of Europe. Songs, such as "Salted Meats and Pickled Beets," "Marching to the Crusades," and "Pillory on the Village Green" entertain and instruct. Each is accompanied by detailed background information and assessments. The rhymes can be used as a complete set, independently, or in varied combinations—whatever suits your needs.

Not only do students gain factual knowledge, they also become active learners as they research and discover a variety of subjects from the medieval period. All student materials are reproducible and designed to help you, the busy teacher.

With the *Setting the Stage* pages, students in grades 4 through 8 can read the information either orally or silently and complete the paired worksheets independently or as a group. Sometimes reading them aloud reinforces understanding and generates good discussions. Children in grades 4 and 5 may need some vocabulary discussion before they begin. At the end of this section is a list of books that provide even more information on these topics.

If you are using the book as a supplement to a text, you may choose to use only one or two of the *Setting the Stage* sheets and accompanying papers. Your curriculum needs will determine which exercises you pick.

Learning stations can start with one poem and its worksheet, or you can have several grouped together. Make answer cards for students to check their own work, or assign a teacher's helper to the task. Follow the work with a "research on your own" activity, too, using the reference or computer section of the library.

Place *Setting the Stage* selections on students' desks the first thing in the morning. Pupils in grades 4 through 8 can "wake up" their brains while you prepare for the day.

Also, if you are not producing the play, give the music instructor two, three, or more of the songs to try in class. The music teacher might even want copies of *Setting the Stage* to create discussion on how the melodies and tempos of the songs match the background information. This is fun and educational for all ages. Written work can be followed-up in either area.

In the *Research and Discovery* activities, teacher guidance for grades 4 and 5 will be needed for students to understand some of the concepts. For instance, talk about facts and opinions and have the class think of some concrete examples before assigning *Johann Gutenberg Was the Best Inventor*. Or discuss the table of information, and then allow children to complete *Black Death Comparison Table, Parts I & II*. Who were King Arthur, Merlin, and Lady Guinevere? Build interest and let students discuss the parts of a story before undertaking the project. Students in grade 6 and above might benefit from interest building, too, but should be able to do the activities on their own. Younger students will need to be assisted with some of the vocabulary words. For additional information, older students can research on the Internet, in reference books, or with related materials. Students in grades 4 and 5 will need assistance and guidance as they explore areas of study.

At the end of the book, everything comes together in the educational play. Producing the play for large audiences requires help from adult volunteers for all age levels. However, students in grades 7 and 8 can take charge of staging the play for a class. It is a great experience.

The book is divided into two sections: Teacher Resources and the Play.

TEACHER RESOURCES includes

- ten original songs and rhymes that can be sung or read.
- detailed background information, *Setting the Stage,* and accompanying worksheets for each song.
- three vocabulary lists—Medieval Figures, Medieval Terms, and Castle Terms—with supplementary student worksheets.
- high-interest research and discovery activities that accommodate a variety of learning styles.
- many ideas for curriculum expansions.
- Gifted and Talented program suggestions.

The PLAY includes

- a musical program containing all ten original songs and rhymes with a finale song.
- exciting characters such as Herald the Dragon that make the Middle Ages fun to learn.
- a script that can be read silently, acted aloud in class, or performed for an audience.
- staging suggestions with everything needed to put on a full production, from cast lists and prop diagrams to costume ideas and performance tips.
- a Teacher Management section that has helpful timesavers like letters to send to parents, prop checklists, notation papers, and even more fun student activities.

In the Final Details section, we have included an Additional Reading List for students wanting to further their studies. For anyone with a love of stories and novels, there are a number of fictional works on this list, all set in the Middle Ages.

We said in the beginning that flexibility is our favorite element of the *In the Middle of the Middle Ages* book. Use any or every part of the text that you want. And back to the original question, "Where do I start?" Wherever *you* choose!

Standards Correlations Introduction

Important content standards include *Building a United States History Curriculum* from the National Council for History Education at www.nche.net and *Expectations of Excellence: Curriculum Standards for Social Studies* from the National Council for the Social Studies at www.ncss.org.

Specific correlations for this resource book to academic content standards are listed for the following sources:

> **History**—*National Standards for History, Basic Edition,* from the National Center for History in the Schools, University of California, Los Angeles
>
> **Language Arts**—*Standards for the English Language Arts*, a Project of the National Council of Teachers of English & International Reading Association
>
> **Arts Education**—*National Standards for Arts Education: Dance, Music, Theatre, Visual Arts: What Every Young American Should Know and Be Able to Do in the Arts* developed by the Consortium of National Arts Education Associations

Using the language arts standards makes *In the Middle of the Middle Ages* a true cross-curriculum activity. Find out more at the National Council of Teachers of English Web site at www.ncte.org.

With the production of the musical, the opportunities to meet content standards for arts education are nearly limitless. Get creative and meet even more standards than those listed. Order the arts education standards at the National Association for Music Education Web site at www.menc.org.

Information for ordering the *National Standards for History, Basic Edition* can be found at http://nchs.ucla.edu.

Text Correlations with National Standards for History

Standards in History for Grades K–4*

TOPIC 4

The History of Peoples of Many Cultures Around the World

Standard 7: Selected attributes and historical developments of various societies in Africa, the Americas, Asia, and Europe.

Standard 8: Major discoveries in science and technology, their social and economic effects, and the scientists and inventors responsible for them.

PAGES	RESOURCE TITLES	STANDARDS
13	Middle Ages Overview	7-A, 7-B, 8-A, 8-B, 8-C
20	Illuminations	7-A, 8-A, 8-C
23	Traveling Minstrel	7-A, 8-C
25	Salted Meats and Pickled Beets	7-A, 8-A
29	Marching to the Crusades	7-A, 7-B, 8-B
33	Sun Up, Sun Down	7-A, 7-B, 8-A
36	Sir Richard, Child to Knight	7-A
39	Pillory on the Village Green	7-A, 8-C
42	Castle in Motion	7-A, 8-A
45	This Riddle	7-A, 8-C
49	Two Cows	7-A
52	Castle Terms—Vocabulary	7-A, 8-A
56	Medieval Terms—Vocabulary	7-A, 7-B, 8-A
60	Medieval Figures—Vocabulary	7-B, 8-A, 8-C
70	Who's Who around the Table	7-A
72	Books Change History	8-C
73	Perpetual Lamps and Flying Machines	8-A, 8-C
75	Choose Your Weapons	8-C
76	Water, Water Everywhere	7-A, 7-B
77	It's Time	7-A
78	Johann Gutenberg Was the Best Inventor	7-A, 8-A, 8-C
79	Plague or Famine?	7-A, 7-B
81	Tall Cathedrals Touch the Sky	7-A
83	Black Death! Comparison Table, Part I	7-B
84	Black Death! Comparison Table, Part II	7-B
85	A Dragon, Can You Imagine?	7-A

From *In the Middle of the Middle Ages: Integrating Content Standards and the Arts.* By Mary Wheeler and Jill Terlep. Music by Mary Wheeler. Illustrations by Jill Terlep. Westport, CT: Libraries Unlimited/Teacher Ideas Press. Copyright © 2007.

PAGES	RESOURCE TITLES	STANDARDS
86	The Normans Are Coming! Details at Eleven	7-A
87	Read All about It	Selections vary
89	Tournament Adventure	7-A
90	Heraldry, In the Heat of the Battle	7-A
92	Come to the Fair, Part I	7-A, 8-A, 8-C
93	Come to the Fair, Part II	7-A, 8-A, 8-C
94	Come to the Fair, Part III	7-A, 8-A, 8-C
95	Do You Need a Hurdy-Gurdy?	7-A, 8-A, 8-C
96	Picture the Past	Selections vary
98	A Pyramid of Power	7-A
99	In the Spirit of the Moment	7-A
102	Cross Curriculum	Selections vary
125	In the Middle of the Middle Ages, the Play	7-A, 7-B, 8-A, 8-B, 8-C

*Reprinted with permission from the National Center for History in the Schools, UCLA (http://nchs.ucla.edu).

From *In the Middle of the Middle Ages: Integrating Content Standards and the Arts*. By Mary Wheeler and Jill Terlep. Music by Mary Wheeler. Illustrations by Jill Terlep. Westport, CT: Libraries Unlimited/Teacher Ideas Press. Copyright © 2007.

Text Correlations with National Standards for History

United States History Standards for Grades 5–12*

ERA 4: Expanding Zones of Exchange and Encounter, 300-1000 CE
    Standard 1: Imperial crises and their aftermath, 300–700 CE.
    Standard 2: Causes and consequences of the rise of Islamic civilization in the seventh–tenth centuries.
    Standard 4: The search for political, social, and cultural redefinition in Europe, 500–1000 CE.
    Standard 7: Major global trends from 300–1000 CE.

ERA 5: Intensified Hemispheric Interactions, 1000-1500 CE
    Standard 2: The redefining of European society and culture, 1000–1300 CE.
    Standard 5: Patterns of crisis and recovery in Afro-Eurasia, 1300–1450.
    Standard 7: Major global trends from 1000–1500 CE.

ERA 6: The Emergence of the First Global Age, 1450-1770
    Standard 2: The student understands the Renaissance, Reformation, and Catholic Reformation.

PAGE	RESOURCE TITLES	ERAS/STANDARDS
13	Middle, Middle Ages Overview	Era 4: 1-A, 1-B, 4-A, 4-B, 7, Era 5: 2-A, 2-B, 2-C, 7
20	Illuminations	Era 4: 4-A; Era 5: 2-C; Era 6: 2-B
23	Traveling Minstrel	Era 5: 2-A, 2-C
25	Salted Meats and Pickled Beets	Era 5: 2-A
29	Marching to the Crusades	Era 4: 2-A; Era 5: 2-A, 2-B
33	Sun Up, Sun Down	Era 4: 4-B; Era 5: 2-A; Era 6: 2-A
36	Sir Richard, Child to Knight	Era 5: 2-A, 2-C
39	Pillory on the Village Green	Era 5: 2-A, 2-C
42	Castle in Motion	Era 5: 2-C
45	This Riddle	Era 5: 2-B; Era 6: 2-B
49	Two Cows	Era 5: 2-A
52	Castle Terms—Vocabulary	Era 5: 2-A
56	Medieval Terms—Vocabulary	Era 4: 1-A, 2-A, 4-A, 4-B; Era 5: 2-A, 2-B, 2-C
60	Medieval Figures—Vocabulary	Era 1: 1-A; Era 5: 2-B, 2-C; Era 6: 2-B
70	Who's Who around the Table	Era 5: 2-C
72	Books Change History	Era 6: 2-B
73	Perpetual Lamps and Flying Machines	Era 5: 2-C
75	Choose Your Weapons	Era 5: 2-A
76	Water, Water Everywhere	Era 4: 1-A, 7
77	It's Time	Era 4: 2-A, Era 5: 2-C
78	Johann Gutenberg Was the Best Inventor	Era 6: 2-B

From In the Middle of the Middle Ages: Integrating Content Standards and the Arts. *By Mary Wheeler and Jill Terlep. Music by Mary Wheeler. Illustrations by Jill Terlep. Westport, CT: Libraries Unlimited/Teacher Ideas Press. Copyright © 2007.*

PAGES	RESOURCE TITLES	ERAS/STANDARDS
79	Plague or Famine?	Era 5: 5-A, 5-B
81	Tall Cathedrals Touch the Sky	Era 5: 2-C
83	Black Death! Comparison Table, Part I	Era 5: 5-A, 5-B
84	Black Death! Comparison Table, Part II	Era 5: 5-A, 5-B
85	A Dragon, Can You Imagine?	Era 5: 2-C
86	The Normans Are Coming! Details at Eleven	Era 5: 2-A
87	Read All about It	Selections Vary
89	Tournament Adventure	Era 5: 2-A
90	Heraldry, In the Heat of the Battle	Era 5: 2-A
92	Come to the Fair, Part I	Era 5: 2-B
93	Come to the Fair, Part II	Era 5: 2-B
94	Come to the Fair, Part III	Era 5: 2-B
95	Do You Need a Hurdy-Gurdy?	Era 5: 2-A
96	Picture the Past	Selections Vary
98	A Pyramid of Power	Era 5: 2-A
99	In the Spirit of the Moment	Era 4: 1-B, 1-C, 2-A, 2-B
102	Cross Curriculum	Selections Vary
125	In the Middle of the Middle Ages, the Play	Era 5: 2-A, 2-B, 2-C

*Reprinted with permission from the National Center for History in the Schools, UCLA (http://nchs.ucla.edu).

Text Correlations with Standards for the English Language Arts
National Council of Teachers of English/International Reading Association*

"A strong grasp of content in the English language arts is vital, but knowledge alone is of little value if one has no need to, or cannot, apply it. The ability to use language for a variety of purposes is therefore another essential part of the learning experience. We believe that a central goal of English language arts education is to ensure that students are able to use language to address their own needs as well as the needs of their families, their communities, and the greater society. In particular, we recommend a focus in English language arts education on four purposes of language use: for obtaining and communicating information, for literary response and expression, for learning and reflection, and for problem solving and application."

PAGES	RESOURCE TITLES	STANDARDS
13	Middle Ages Overview	1, 2, 3
20	Illuminations	1, 2, 3, 4, 5, 6
23	Traveling Minstrel	1, 2, 3, 4, 5, 6
25	Salted Meats and Pickled Beets	1, 2, 3, 4, 5, 6
29	Marching to the Crusades	1, 2, 3
33	Sun Up, Sun Down	1, 2, 3, 4, 5, 6, 12
36	Sir Richard, Child to Knight	1, 2, 3, 4, 5, 6, 11
39	Pillory on the Village Green	1, 2, 3
42	Castle in Motion	1, 2, 3, 4, 5, 6, 12
45	This Riddle	1, 2, 3, 4, 5, 6
49	Two Cows	1, 2, 3, 4, 5, 6
52	Castle Terms—Vocabulary	1, 2, 3, 4, 5, 6
56	Medieval Terms—Vocabulary	1, 2, 3, 4, 5, 6
60	Medieval Figures—Vocabulary	1, 2, 3, 4, 5, 6
70	Who's Who around the World	1, 2, 3, 4, 5, 6, 9, 12
72	Books Change History	1, 2, 3, 4, 5, 6
73	Perpetual Lamps and Flying Machines	1, 2, 3, 4, 5, 6, 7, 8, 12
75	Choose Your Weapons	4, 5, 6
76	Water, Water Everywhere	1, 2, 3, 4, 5, 6
77	It's Time	1, 2, 3
78	Johann Gutenberg Was the Best Inventor	3
79	Plague or Famine?	1, 2, 3, 4, 5, 6, 7, 8
81	Tall Cathedrals Touch the Sky	1, 2, 3, 8
83	Black Death Comparison Table, Part I	1
84	Black Death Comparison Table, Part II	3, 5, 8
85	A Dragon, Can You Imagine?	12

From In the Middle of the Middle Ages: Integrating Content Standards and the Arts. By Mary Wheeler and Jill Terlep. Music by Mary Wheeler. Illustrations by Jill Terlep. Westport, CT: Libraries Unlimited/Teacher Ideas Press. Copyright © 2007.

PAGES	RESOURCE TITLES	STANDARDS
86	The Normans Are Coming! Details at Eleven	3, 4, 5, 6, 8, 9, 11, 12
87	Read All about It	1, 2, 3, 4, 5, 6
89	Tournament Adventure	4, 5, 6
90	Heraldry, In the Heat of the Battle	3, 4, 7, 8
92	Come to the Fair, Part I	1
93	Come to the Fair, Part II	9, 11, 12
94	Come to the Fair, Part III	5
95	Do You Need a Hurdy-Gurdy?	1, 4, 5, 6, 7, 8, 12
96	Picture the Past	1, 2, 3, 6
98	A Pyramid of Power	1, 4, 5, 6
99	In the Spirit of the Moment	1, 2, 3, 4, 5, 6, 9, 12
102	Cross Curriculum	Selections Vary
125	In the Middle of the Middle Ages, the Play	1, 2, 3, 11, 12

* Copyright 1996 by the International Reading Association and the National Council of Teachers of English. Published by the International Reading Association and the National Council of Teachers of English, reprinted with permission.

From In the Middle of the Middle Ages: Integrating Content Standards and the Arts. By Mary Wheeler and Jill Terlep. Music by Mary Wheeler. Illustrations by Jill Terlep. Westport, CT: Libraries Unlimited/Teacher Ideas Press. Copyright © 2007.

Text Correlations with National Standards for Arts Education

National Standards for Arts Education:
Dance, Music, Theatre, Visual Arts*

"All peoples, everywhere, have an abiding need for meaning—to connect time and space, experience and event, body and spirit, intellect and emotion. People create art to make these connections, to express the otherwise inexpressible. A society and a people without the arts are unimaginable."

For Grades K–4 and Grades 5–8

PAGES	RESOURCE TITLES	CONTENT STANDARDS
20	Illuminations	Visual Arts 1, 3, 4, 6
23	Traveling Minstrel	Music 4
52	Castle Terms—Vocabulary	Visual Arts 1, 3, 4
76	Water, Water Everywhere	Theatre 1, 2, 3, 5
81	Tall Cathedrals Touch the Sky	Visual Arts 2, 3, 4, 5, 6
85	A Dragon, Can You Imagine?	Visual Arts 1, 2, 3, 4
86	The Normans Are Coming! Details at Eleven	Theatre 8
94	Come to the Fair, Part III	Visual Arts 1, 2, 3, 4
96	Picture the Past	Visual Arts 2, 3, 4
102	Cross Curriculum, Varied Selections	Music (all) Visual Arts (all)
125	In the Middle of the Middle Ages, the Play, Grades K–4	Dance 1, 2, 3, 4, 5, 6, 7 Music 1, 2, 3, 5, 6, 7, 8, 9 Theatre 2, 3, 4, 7
125	In the Middle of the Middle Ages, the Play, Grades 5–8	Dance 1, 2, 3, 4, 5, 6, 7 Music 1, 2, 5, 6, 7, 8, 9 Theatre 2, 3, 4, 6, 7, 8

* From *National Standards for Arts Education*. Copyright © 1994 by Music Educators National Conference (MENC). Used by permission. The complete National Arts Standards and additional materials relating to the Standards are available from MENC—The National Association for Music Education, 1806 Robert Fulton Drive, Reston, VA 20191.

Teacher Resources

*Background Information and Rhymes,
Guided Activities*

Song and Rhyme Synopsis

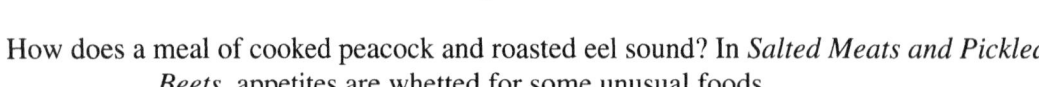

How does a meal of cooked peacock and roasted eel sound? In *Salted Meats and Pickled Beets,* appetites are whetted for some unusual foods.

The *Traveling Minstrel* performs again just for the lords and ladies and families of today. Listen to those "tales of battlefield glories."

Get ready for lots of action with *Castle in Motion*. Every stage and choir member does aerobic movements that match the activities of medieval times. So "swim the moat" and "scale the wall" to the exciting times.

From *Sun Up, Sun Down,* join the peasant and his wife as they struggle in the fields of the castle's shadow.

Parade along with the Crusader and his horse, of course. Armor weighs a lot, but that won't stop any good steed from *Marching to the Crusades.*

Illuminations—let's light up minds with knowledge and celebrate the intricate decorations on the pages of long ago.

It was a crime he didn't mean, so pity the poor man in the *Pillory on the Village Green.* Don't tease him, though.

Solve *This Riddle* and learn of Leonardo (Leo) Pisano's number symbols. Everyone needs to count his or her blessings.

Could *Two Cows* really know if the bride is happy? Maybe the rest of her dowry—a boar, seven sows, and three big draught horses—will tell more.

Say his name along with him, and be proud of it in *Sir Richard, Child to Knight.*

Middle Ages Overview

Middle Ages Years

The Middle Ages in Europe are generally referred to as the years after the fall of the Roman Empire up to the beginning of the Renaissance, approximately 500 AD to 1400–1500. The years are also noted as the Early Middle Ages (500–900/1000), High Middle Ages (900/1000–1300), and Late Middle Ages (1300–1500).

Roman Empire

For several hundred years, the Roman Empire provided stability, security, and prosperity for its citizens. With its superior system of roads, the central government maintained communications and control over all parts of its state. Constructed of stones on solid foundations, the roads traveled straight routes from one site to another. Even bridges over rivers were expertly built. Well-trained armies could be sent to settle invasions or attacks. Law and order prevailed.

However, even the Roman Empire was not invincible. For many years, various German tribes had been migrating into Roman territories. The Visigoth tribal chieftain, Alaric, marched on Rome in 410 AD, and the defeated Roman Empire began falling apart.

Many years of devastating wars followed. Growing in place of the strong central government was the manorial system with its lords and castles and thousands of unconnected villages—only uninhabited land and forest lay between them. The new town sites were almost always located on the shores of rivers and streams because of their resources.

Feudal System

With the collapse of the Roman Empire, people needed protection from barbarian attacks. A political system, labeled centuries later as *feudalism,* emerged and evolved in varying ways in Europe.

At the top of the feudal pyramid was the king who granted parcels of his land, or fiefs, to entrusted noblemen or vassals. In return, the vassals promised their "fealty" or loyalty and to serve their lord in war. The most powerful noblemen were barons, earls, and counts. They often controlled lesser nobles or knights, who also received land and a feudal contract in exchange for protection. At the base of the pyramid were the workers, peasants, and serfs.

The Church, with its tracts of land, was a part of the feudal system. Abbots and bishops became vassals of the king and great noblemen.

Members of the feudal society, whose knights defended the order, practiced chivalry and its code of values. With the Church, castles and their outer lands made up the feudal estates.

From In the Middle of the Middle Ages: Integrating Content Standards and the Arts. By Mary Wheeler and Jill Terlep. Music by Mary Wheeler. Illustrations by Jill Terlep. Westport, CT: Libraries Unlimited/Teacher Ideas Press. Copyright © 2007.

William the Conqueror

After crossing the English Channel in October 1066, William, the duke of Normandy, landed several thousand troops in England. From northern France, the Normans battled fiercely and defeated the Saxon army at the Battle of Hastings. William the Conqueror was formally crowned king of England on Christmas Day in 1066, and he introduced the feudal system to the country.

Castles were built in all major towns, and William's loyal Norman followers gained the Anglo-Saxon lands. In a short amount of time, a survey of the resources and landownership of England, *The Domesday Book,* was written. The Normans learned a lot from the information.

Henry I

Born in 1068, Henry I was the son of William the Conqueror. From 1100 to 1135 Henry reigned as king of England. He was interested in making his position as ruler stronger. Henry's administrator organized the government so that it operated much more efficiently. The treasury department was named the Exchequer, and its system made it much easier to decide how much money should be collected.

Henry II

The grandson of Henry I, Henry II. was born in 1133 and died in 1189. He married the ex-wife of Louis VII of France after he met her in Paris. Crowned in 1154, Henry II ruled firmly but not harshly. During his reign, a sworn jury of twelve witnessing men were used to deal with criminal activities. His changes in laws were incorporated into the legal system in England and eventually the United States. One failure that Henry II suffered was the death of his one-time friend, churchman Thomas Becket. Four of Henry's knights murdered Becket, who was later canonized as a saint.

Richard the Lion-Hearted

Richard the Lion-Hearted, 1157–1199, was known as a mighty warrior. Ignoring his job as ruler, he focused his efforts on fighting. To free Jerusalem from Muslim control, Richard set off on the Crusade. Richard returned to England in 1194 briefly only to leave again. He died on the Continent trying to regain land for England that had been lost. His reign lasted from 1189 to 1199.

King John and the Magna Carta

John, 1167 to 1216, was the brother of Richard the Lion-Hearted. Crowned king of England in 1199 after Richard's death, John was forced to sign the Magna Carta (Great Charter). The powerful lords, with the support of the Church, were unhappy with John's rule. Faced with enormous debts, King John had raised taxes. Under his reign, a civil war also resulted in the loss of most of the French possessions, including Normandy, across the Channel.

King John was presented with the Magna Carta on June 15, 1215, at Runnymeade, outside of London. Eventually, the document became the basis of the modern English constitution. The Magna Carta bound the king to observe common law and tradition and led to democratic freedoms.

Henry III

Henry III, 1207–1272, succeeded his father, King John, to the throne in 1216. He assumed his duties as king in 1216 and continued until 1272. The feudal government that he inherited was not well organized, and during his reign, money problems were dominant.

Crusades

On November 18, 1095, Pope Urban II spoke to a crowd in southern France. In his speech, he urged the people to retake the Holy Land from the Muslims. The Christians, known as Crusaders, set out for Jerusalem in 1096. The first Crusaders were masses of people from all walks of life, and they gained control of Jerusalem. In 1212, thousands of boys and girls set off for the Holy Land in the Children's Crusade. In all, there were eight Crusades (some sources say nine) in a little over 200 years, lasting until the early 1300s.

Knighthood

At about the age of seven years, a young noble boy went to another manor to begin his preparation for knighthood. There he began his academic, religious, and physical education. As he got older, he started basic training in weaponry.

Next, he became a squire, and he was assigned to serve a knight and learn from him. Codes of chivalry were taught. Studies continued with more emphasis on military skills. When the squire finally was dubbed a knight in a religious ceremony, he swore his allegiance and loyalty or fealty. Skilled in warfare, he promised to serve his lord in the feudal system. Before the 13th century, for protection in battle, the knight wore chain mail, which was a long shirt and leggings, made of layers of steel rings.

Tournaments

At times when they were not engaged in actual warfare, tournaments provided a setting for knights to practice and display their skills and courage. Even though they were games, it was not uncommon for participants to be accidentally injured or even killed. Mock battles were favorite pastimes for noble families. Competitors showed off their obedience to a code of love and honor.

Village Fairs

Village fairs took place once or twice a year. Held outside the castle walls, they were important for the trade they attracted and the activities they provided. Traveling merchants set up tents and bargained. A variety of entertainers like musicians, jugglers, and acrobats performed. Dancing bears and trained animals put on shows. The occasions were very popular with the villagers.

Education

Monastic and cathedral schools were earlier centers for learning, but universities began appearing in Europe during the 12th and 13th centuries. Growth of towns and increased trade hastened the renewed interest in knowledge. Classic works of Aristotle and others stimulated more intellectual pursuits. New scientific, astronomical, and mathematical information reaching Europe from the East also spurred academic curiosities.

Cathedrals

The building of churches or cathedrals was the great work of the Middle Ages. Stonecutters, sculptors, and many other craftsmen labored for decades or even centuries to build the magnificent structures. Touching the skies, the cathedrals included elaborate stained glass windows, sculptures, and statues that told the story of Christianity. Employing classic Romanesque and Gothic styles of architectures, the buildings stand today as monuments to the workers' skills and to this important period in history.

From *In the Middle of the Middle Ages: Integrating Content Standards and the Arts.* By Mary Wheeler and Jill Terlep. Music by Mary Wheeler. Illustrations by Jill Terlep. Westport, CT: Libraries Unlimited/Teacher Ideas Press. Copyright © 2007.

Illuminations—In the Middle of the Middle Ages

(Chorus)
Illuminations are decorations on the pages of the books of yesterday.
Illuminations—Learn information.
Let us see how others used to work and play.

(Verses)
A law and order government—they organized it well.
Their principles lived on although the Roman Empire fell.
Years of devastating wars
Passed as towns grew on the shores
In the middle of the Middle Ages.

A Conqueror named William, ten sixty-six was crowned.
His ruthlessness and courage throughout Europe were renowned.
Into England, Norman's came;
Lots of land the Duke would claim
In the middle of the Middle Ages.

Ten ninety-five's when Christians began the First Crusade.
A journey to Jerusalem to win it back was made.
Eight Crusades, two hundred years –
Even children volunteered
In the middle of the Middle Ages.

His loyalty and service were promised to a lord.
The knight, a mighty warrior, could fight with lance and sword.
First, a page and then a squire,
Chain mail was his safe attire
In the middle of the Middle Ages.

From *In the Middle of the Middle Ages: Integrating Content Standards and the Arts.* By Mary Wheeler and Jill Terlep. Music by Mary Wheeler. Illustrations by Jill Terlep. Westport, CT: Libraries Unlimited/Teacher Ideas Press. Copyright © 2007.

*The tournaments provided a show where knights were trained.
Magnificent occasions—noble families entertained.
Everyone liked village fairs.
Merchants came and sold their wares
In the middle of the Middle Ages.
A pyramid of power—the king was at the top.
Below him came the vassals, knights, and serfs who farmed the crops.
As the strong protected weak,
Feudalism reached its peak
In the middle of the Middle Ages.*

*King John had opposition; he went to Runnymede.
He signed the Magna Carta, but reluctantly agreed.
Twelve fifteen was when they met.
Liberties were what they'd get
In the middle of the Middle Ages.*

*A Lion-Hearted Richard and Henrys one, two, three
Were all among the heirs who served as English royalty.
With education on the rise,
Tall cathedrals touched the skies
In the middle of the Middle Ages.*

NAME _____ DATE_____

Middle Ages Review Questions

1. The Middle Ages generally are described as starting after the fall of what?

2. They lasted until the beginning of what age?

3. What empire built a superior system of roads?

4. What tribes migrated for years into Roman territories before the empire fell?

5. Identify the Visigoth tribal chieftain who marched on Rome in 410 AD.

6. What is the name of the landed system that replaced the strong, Roman central government?

7. Near what geographic features were new towns always located in the Middle Ages?

8. Who was the leader of the English invasion in 1066?

9. What is the historians' nickname for the duke of Normandy?

10. From what area did the Normans originate?

11. What body of water did William the Conqueror cross to invade England?

12. What is the title of the Norman survey book of English land ownership in the eleventh century?

13. What religious leader urged the crowd to retake the Holy Land in 1095?

14. In what year did the Christians set out for the Holy Land in the First Crusade?

15. How many Crusades were there in all?

16. Over how many years did the Crusades last?

17. About what age did a young noble boy begin his preparation for knighthood?

18. What is a long shirt and leggings, made of layers of steel rings, called?

19. What events provided the knights an opportunity to display their courage and skills?

20. How often did village fairs take place?

21. Name the political system that emerged for the protection of the people after the collapse of the Roman Empire.

22. Who was at the top of the feudal pyramid?

23. Who was at the base of the feudal pyramid?

24. What important document was King John forced to sign?

25. When did King John sign the document?

26. Whose knights murdered churchman Thomas Becket?

27. What English monarch was known as a mighty warrior?

28. During what centuries did the universities begin appearing in Europe?

29. Which buildings that were constructed during the Middle Ages still stand as their great monuments?

30. Whose story was told by the stained glass windows, sculptures, and statues in the cathedrals?

From In the Middle of the Middle Ages: Integrating Content Standards and the Arts. By Mary Wheeler and Jill Terlep. Music by Mary Wheeler. Illustrations by Jill Terlep. Westport, CT: Libraries Unlimited/Teacher Ideas Press. Copyright © 2007.

Illuminations

Setting the Stage

Before the invention of the printing press by Johann Gutenberg of Germany in the mid-1400s, books were reproduced by hand. In the monasteries, monks labored for weeks and years to copy and transcribe the Bible and other religious writings, as well as important works of philosophy, science, mathematics, and astronomy.

Manuscripts were written on parchment or vellum (animal skin), not paper. When the hand-printed texts were finished, they were painted with ornate decorations. Sometimes the monks themselves made the drawings, but illuminators completed the figures in other books. The illuminations were intricately drawn with great attention to detail. The creators often experimented with the shades they used for these very colorful artworks.

Title pages of books were illuminated, and the decorated initial, the first letter of the first word, was used to draw attention to a page or concept in the text. Decorations were also made along the margins of the pages. Illuminated drawings often told stories. Many of the books were religious, but there were lots of legal, courtly, and academic texts that were elaborately adorned, too.

Cathedral schools were early centers for learning. In the monasteries, the monks searched for truths, especially with regard to religion.

Later in the Middle Ages, there was a renewed interest in education. Growth of villages brought attention to the need for knowledge. More trained men were required for administering the affairs of the villages and their increasing populations. Revival of the works of classic Greek philosophers such as Aristotle promoted scholarship. Crusaders, returning from their military journeys, brought news of educational advances and discoveries in the Islamic and Byzantine worlds. Arab countries had never stopped their pursuit of learning, and new information of Arabic numerals, astronomical findings, and scientific growth reached and stimulated learning in Europe.

Universities began appearing in Europe during the Middle Ages. The University of Paris and Notre Dame were renowned as centers for learning. In England, Oxford and Cambridge had their beginnings in the early 12th century. Oxford was a leading school attended by scholars such as Roger Bacon and John Wyclif. Religion, arithmetic, grammar, dialogue, rhetoric, geometry, astronomy, Latin, music, law, and medicine were among the subjects that were studied.

Illuminations

Illuminations are decorations on the pages of the books of yesterday.
Illuminations—Learn information.
Let us see how others used to work and play.

From In the Middle of the Middle Ages: Integrating Content Standards and the Arts. By Mary Wheeler and Jill Terlep. Music by Mary Wheeler. Illustrations by Jill Terlep. Westport, CT: Libraries Unlimited/Teacher Ideas Press. Copyright © 2007.

NAME _____ DATE _____

Illuminations

Before the invention of the printing press, manuscripts were copied by hand. It took a long time to transcribe books, and very few people owned them. However, if you lived in the Middle Ages and could have <u>any three</u> books as yours, which would you choose? The books can be from the past or present. Explain why you selected them.

1. _____
   _____
   _____
   _____
   _____
   _____
   _____

2. _____
   _____
   _____
   _____
   _____
   _____
   _____

3. _____
   _____
   _____
   _____
   _____
   _____
   _____

From In the Middle of the Middle Ages: Integrating Content Standards and the Arts. *By Mary Wheeler and Jill Terlep. Music by Mary Wheeler. Illustrations by Jill Terlep. Westport, CT: Libraries Unlimited/Teacher Ideas Press. Copyright © 2007.*

Draw your own illumination. It can be an initial to a first word, a margin decoration, or a title page drawing. Use colors, and add a lot of details in the figures.

Traveling Minstrel

Setting the Stage

Playing harps, lutes, viols, and bagpipes, minstrels traveled to castles and manors entertaining lords, ladies, and their guests. These professional musicians, also called jongleurs, sang of the knights' courage, honor, and heroism in battles. Feats were often exaggerated, and in real life, the knights did not always live up to the deeds described in the minstrels' music. Songs and stories of love and chivalry were also popular.

In the great hall of the castle, after the meals and the minstrels' performances, guests, such as knights or barons, sometimes joined in the musical celebrations. Accompanied by the minstrels with a chord or background, visitors composed and sang their own songs for the company. Some danced to the music, too.

Because books were rare and few people could read, the minstrels provided a welcome diversion to the castle occupants. In exchange for performing, the musicians were provided food, lodging, and sometimes other gifts, such as clothes.

Musical notation was not widely practiced or perfected until years later, so very few of the minstrels' songs remain in existence today. Most tunes were memorized or improvised by the entertainers, and although they were sometimes sung for hundreds of years, they were unfortunately never written down.

Traveling Minstrel

A traveling minstrel, my job is to sing. From castle to manor I go.
I entertain ladies and lords and their guests. Always, I put on a good show.

While the people are feasting, I am singing my songs.
Later, all of them dance to music I play along.

A traveling minstrel, my job is to sing. From castle to manor I go.
I entertain ladies and lords and their guests. Always, I put on a good show.

They all like to hear stories of knights and chivalrous ways.
Tales of battlefield glories brighten my listeners' days.

A traveling minstrel, my job is to sing. From castle to manor I go.
I entertain ladies and lords and their guests. Always, I put on a good show.

Show respect to the ladies. Prove your honor is true.
Bravely fight for your manor; that's what noblemen do.

From In the Middle of the Middle Ages: Integrating Content Standards and the Arts. *By Mary Wheeler and Jill Terlep. Music by Mary Wheeler. Illustrations by Jill Terlep. Westport, CT: Libraries Unlimited/Teacher Ideas Press. Copyright © 2007.*

NAME _____ DATE _____

Traveling Minstrel

Fill in blanks with the correct answers. Make sure to spell each word correctly.

1. Minstrels, also called _ _ _ _ _ _ _ _ _ _ , were professional musicians who sang of the knights' courage and honor.

2. The entertainers traveled to _ _ _ _ _ _ _ and _ _ _ _ _ _ _ to entertain lords, ladies, and their guests.

3. The minstrels often _ _ _ _ _ _ _ _ _ _ _ _ the courageous deeds of the knights.

4. Guests were entertained in the _ _ _ _ _ _ _ _ _ , a room in the castle.

5. Sometimes the guests, _ _ _ _ _ _ _ _ _ or _ _ _ _ _ _ _ , joined in and sang their own songs.

6. In exchange for performing, musicians were provided _ _ _ _ and _ _ _ _ _ _ _ .

7. Because _ _ _ _ _ _ were rare, minstrels were welcomed to the manors and castles.

8. Few of the minstrels' _ _ _ _ _ remain in existence today.

9. Most tunes were _ _ _ _ _ _ _ _ _ _ by the entertainers.

10. Knights must show _ _ _ _ _ _ _ _ to the ladies.

Write one or two verses to the *Traveling Minstrel* poem.

_____
_____
_____
_____
_____
_____
_____
_____
_____

From *In the Middle of the Middle Ages: Integrating Content Standards and the Arts.* By Mary Wheeler and Jill Terlep. Music by Mary Wheeler. Illustrations by Jill Terlep. Westport, CT: Libraries Unlimited/Teacher Ideas Press. Copyright © 2007.

Salted Meats and Pickled Beets

Setting the Stage

During the Middle Ages, a castle needed to be well stocked with provisions. Many visitors and even groups of soldiers were often fed there on short notice. Having ample food reserves on hand was essential during times of battle. As a means of warfare, enemy soldiers would cut off the castle's food supply and destroy its crops, and palace residents had to live for long periods of time within the castle walls. Stored rations fed the inhabitants until the conflicts were resolved.

Several cooks in a huge kitchen prepared meals served in the castle. Carcasses of meat were turned and roasted on a spit over a fire, and huge cauldrons, layered with different foods such as fish and puddings, simmered beside the meats.

A wide variety of meats was served during various feasts in the great hall. Pork, bacon, mutton, beef, duck, salmon, cod, herring, chicken, venison—lords and ladies ate a lot of these. Even exotic dishes such as pheasant, partridge, eel, and peacock were elaborately prepared.

Because of the lack of refrigeration, food needed to be preserved. Salting, smoking, or drying meat and fish kept them edible. Expensive salt, made from evaporated seawater, helped save meats for the winter. Heavy spices and pungent vegetables such as onions and garlic were frequently used to cover the foods' stale flavors and spoilage. Other flavorings, including fruits and honey, were used to mask tastes.

Because raw fruits and vegetables were considered unhealthy, many were pickled in brine, which is salty water. Milk products were turned into salted butter and hard cheese. Wine, pressed from grapes, was stored for the lord and nobility, but common people drank weak ale, cider, or water. Even the water had to be flavored from its stale taste by adding honey or licorice to it.

At the lord's windmill, flour was ground. Bread, an important staple, was baked in large brick ovens. Using wooden shovels, or peels, the loaves were removed from the oven to cool. On some grounds, castles had bakehouses owned by the lord. Villagers could buy coarse, brown bread there, but fine bread was reserved for the lord's dining.

Because forks were not yet used as eating utensils, meals were eaten with fingers, or a knife and spoon. Dinners were served on pewter plates or on trenchers. The trenchers, which were heavy, thick slices of the coarse, brown bread, soaked up sauces and grease. If a diner was especially hungry, he could eat part of the dish. Uneaten trenchers were often given away to beggars and dogs after their use in the hall.

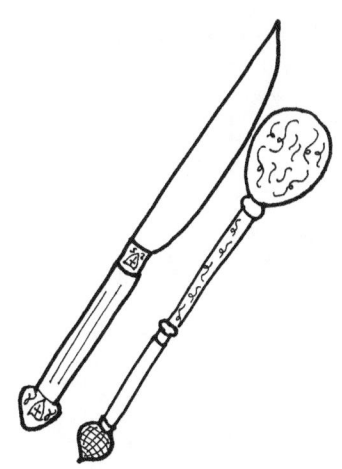

From In the Middle of the Middle Ages: Integrating Content Standards and the Arts. *By Mary Wheeler and Jill Terlep. Music by Mary Wheeler. Illustrations by Jill Terlep. Westport, CT: Libraries Unlimited/Teacher Ideas Press. Copyright © 2007.*

Dragons are mythical creatures, especially popular in tales about the Middle Ages. Usually large, lizard-like, and ferocious, the medieval European dragons often guarded treasures in caves, mountains, lakes, or dens. In the fictional stories, brave heroes often slew the dragons and gained their wealth.

Salted Meats and Pickled Beets

Hungry Herald! Hungry Herald!
But my favorite when I'm fed, have I said, is bread.

I eat what all the castle eats
Like bacon, cod, and salted meats.
Pheasant, partridge, mutton, hare—
Their spicy odors fill the air.

Hungry Herald! Hungry Herald!
But my favorite when I'm fed, have I said, is bread.

I eat what all the castle eats,
And peacocks are their favorite treats.
Salted butter, eggs, hard cheese—
I often eat a lot of these.

Hungry Herald! Hungry Herald!
But my favorite when I'm fed, have I said, is bread.

I eat what all the castle eats
Like puddings, pears, and pickled beets.
Salmon, honey, apples, stew—
I wash them down with ale I brew.

Hungry Herald! Hungry Herald!
But my favorite when I'm fed, have I said, is bread.

NAME _____ DATE _____

Salted Meats and Pickled Beets

In many ways meals in the Middle Ages were different from those of today, but there were also things that were the same. Think about menus, food preservation, kitchens, eating utensils, cookware, and other facts.

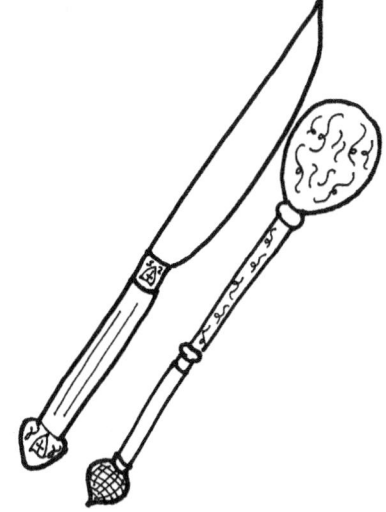

Compare the medieval meals to those in the present. Write five complete sentences telling how they are alike.

(Example: Meat was cooked on a spit over a fire, and on special occasions, we still roast hogs or other meats over a spit.)

1. _____

2. _____

3. _____

4. _____

5. _____

From In the Middle of the Middle Ages: Integrating Content Standards and the Arts. *By Mary Wheeler and Jill Terlep. Music by Mary Wheeler. Illustrations by Jill Terlep. Westport, CT: Libraries Unlimited/Teacher Ideas Press. Copyright © 2007.*

Contrast the meals of both ages. Write five complete sentences telling how they are different.

(Example: Raw fruits and vegetables were considered unhealthy in the Middle Ages, but today we know that they are a crucial part of a balanced diet.)

1. _____
   _____
   _____
   _____

2. _____
   _____
   _____
   _____

3. _____
   _____
   _____
   _____

4. _____
   _____
   _____
   _____

5. _____
   _____
   _____
   _____

Marching to the Crusades

Setting the Stage

Muhammad, the Prophet of Islam, was born in the Arabian city of Mecca in 570 AD. After hearing revelations from God, he began preaching the worship of one god only and of the Last Judgment.

His religious reforms and campaigns were received and supported readily, especially by the lower classes. When his followers began to be persecuted, many fled to Ethiopia. Muhammad's migration to Medina in 622 AD is called the *Hijra* and marks the beginning date of the Muslim calendar.

The Prophet returned to Mecca in 630, and he and his followers conquered all of Arabia. He succeeded in uniting all of the Arab tribes into one nation with one religion. Muhammad's final revelation from God is written in the Holy Qur'an. Muhammad died in 633 AD.

Beginning in 1096, the Crusades were a series of wars lasting more than 200 years aimed at recapturing the Holy Land from Muslim control.

Pope Urban II, a Frenchman, appealed to the masses in 1095 and called for the freeing of Jerusalem for Christianity. Following Muhammad's death, the Turks had gained power of the city in the 1070s, and there were reports of Christian mistreatments and persecutions.

In the First Crusade, approximately 30,000 people, from all walks of life, set out to recapture the Holy Land in 1096. They were promised remission from their sins, and "God wills it," was their battle cry. Wearing red crosses with white banners, the Christians captured Jerusalem in the First Crusade. Ultimately, after eight Crusades, Muslims had again regained control by the 1300s.

Horses were the knights' most important instruments of warfare, and learning to ride and care for them began early in the boys' lives. A wealthy knight owned at least two or three horses. Highly trained warhorses from Spain and Italy were expensive but were considered the best. The stallions were used for fighting and tournaments, and they needed to carry their rider and his heavy armor. His other horses were used for carrying baggage or regular riding.

By the middle of the Middle Ages, armor consisted of a helmet, shield, and a coat of chain mail (metal rings linked together). When the duke of Normandy invaded England in 1066, that armor was worn over linen or leather underclothes. Armor weighed approximately 40 to 50 pounds. In the 14th and 15th centuries, knights wore entire suits of body armor, and even horses did, too.

From In the Middle of the Middle Ages: Integrating Content Standards and the Arts. *By Mary Wheeler and Jill Terlep. Music by Mary Wheeler. Illustrations by Jill Terlep. Westport, CT: Libraries Unlimited/Teacher Ideas Press. Copyright © 2007.*

Marching to the Crusades

Following Muhammad's death, a Holy War was waged.
Muslims ruled Jerusalem, and Christians were enraged.

From petty knights to local lords,
Some thousands heard the papal call.
The masses marched in the First Crusade,
'Twas barons, peasants, one and all.

To face their sins and save their souls—
"God wills it!" was their battle cry.
Crusaders marched to the Holy Land
Reclaiming power from days gone by.

(Horse and Knight)
Marching to the Crusades—together we're marching along.
Marching to the Crusades—together we're singing a song.

(Horse) I'm the horse,
(Knight) And I'm the knight.
(Horse) I can prance,
(Knight) And I can fight.

(Horse and Knight)
Marching to the Crusades—together we're marching along.

(Knight)
I tried on my new metal armor.
I hoped to impress a young maid,
But my horse fell down when I got on his back.
(Horse)
He didn't warn me how much armor weighed.

(Horse and Knight)
Marching to the Crusades—together we're marching along.
Marching to the Crusades—together we're singing a song.

(Horse) I'm the horse,
(Knight) And I'm the knight.
(Horse) I can prance,
(Knight) And I can fight.

(Horse and Knight)
Marching to the Crusades—together we're marching along.

From *In the Middle of the Middle Ages: Integrating Content Standards and the Arts.* By Mary Wheeler and Jill Terlep. Music by Mary Wheeler. Illustrations by Jill Terlep. Westport, CT: Libraries Unlimited/Teacher Ideas Press. Copyright © 2007.

Marching to the Crusades

Circle the letter of the correct answer.

1. In the Islamic religion, Muhammad is considered a
   a. priest.   b. prophet.   c. minister.

2. Muhammad was born in the Arabian city of
   a. Jerusalem.   b. Medina.   c. Mecca.

3. Muhammad's religious reforms were received readily by the
   a. lower class. b. middle class. c. upper class.

4. In AD 622, the prophet was forced to migrate to
   a. Mecca.   b. Hijra.   c. Medina.

5. The sacred book of the Islamic religion is called the
   a. Holy Qur'an. b. Holy Bible.   c. Holy Grail.

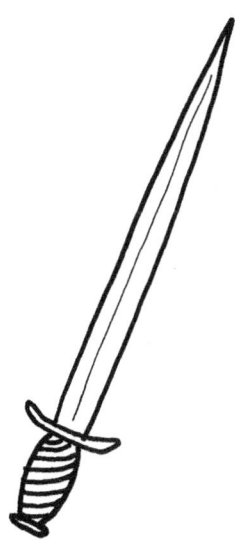

6. The Crusades were a series of wars lasting more than
   a. 200 days.   b. 200 weeks.   c. 200 years.

7. Muhammad and his followers conquered all of
   a. India.   b. Arabia.   c. Ethiopia.

8. The person who appealed to the masses and called for the Crusades was
   a. Muhammad.   b. Pope Urban II. c. Pope John III.

9. After Muhammad's death Jerusalem was ruled by the
   a. Arabians.   b. English.   c. Turks.

10. About 30,000 people from all walks of life marched in the
    a. First Crusade. b. Second Crusade. c. Third Crusade.

11. Those who marched in the Crusades were promised remission from their
    a. sins. b. sickness. c. religion.

12. To identify themselves and their cause, Crusaders wore red crosses with
    a. white sleeves. b. red banners. c. white banners.

13. The first Crusaders began marching in the year
    a. 630 AD. b. 1070 AD. c. 1096 AD.

14. The most important instrument of warfare for a knight was his
    a. helmet. b. horse. c. armor.

15. The best and most highly trained warhorses were from
    a. England. b. Spain and Italy. c. France and Spain.

16. The number of horses that a wealthy knight owned was at least
    a. three. b. five. c. ten.

17. Metal rings linked together, forming a protective coat for the knight, were called
    a. helmet covers. b. ring bearers. c. chain mail.

18. In 1066, the duke of Normandy invaded
    a. England. b. Spain. c. Italy.

19. Metal armor weighed approximately
    a. 90 pounds. b. 70 pounds. c. 50 pounds.

20. "God wills it!" was the battle cry of the
    a. Muslims. b. Crusaders. c. knights.

Sun Up, Sun Down (A Peasant's Life)

Setting the Stage

The peasants lived near the lord's castle, which was usually the largest structure for miles around. Under the strong guard of the castle, the village population grew. In exchange for land and protection from marauding armies, the peasants provided a labor force to work the fields.

Living in a manorial system, based on agriculture, the lord's property was divided into strips. Sun up to sun down, the peasants worked for the lord two or three days a week and for themselves the remainder of the time. They did not work on Sundays or on saints' days. The peasants' land and everything they had belonged to the lord. Besides giving a share of their work, they also paid a yearly rent and taxes on goods, and a fee was charged for grain that had to be ground at the lord's mill. A tithe to the Church was also expected.

Most peasants used wooden tools, edged with metal. Sickles for harvesting corn, scythes for cutting grass, and spades for digging were the primary hand tools. Introduced in the 12th century, plows with iron blades were pulled by draught animals.

Damp and dark, a typical peasant's home was a single room where the family ate and slept. Sometimes during severe winter weather, even animals—geese, pigs, chickens, sheep, and livestock—shared the quarters.

Starting with a timber frame of heavy branches, the walls of the dwellings consisted of wattle—interwoven twigs and sticks—and daub—clay mixed with straw. Roofs were mostly thatched with straw or reeds. A crude hearth was used for heating and cooking, and a hole was cut in the roof to vent the smoke. The packed dirt floor was sometimes covered with straw.

Furniture was scarce, maybe including a rough-hewn table, a storage chest, a loom for weaving, and some three-legged stools. On the floor, the family often slept together in a box filled with straw or dried leaves.

Peasants ate gruel, which is a thin porridge, and pottage, a kind of stew with vegetables and some chunks of meat. Dark, coarse bread, cheese, and whatever garden vegetables the peasants grew were included in their limited and monotonous diet. Utensils were made of wood, pottery, and sometimes metal.

Hunting was prohibited; only the nobility had that right. Poachers—people who hunted or fished illegally on the lord's reserve—were punished.

Women spun wool to make outer garments. Both men and women wore tunics, tied with a leather strap around the waist. In the winter, they wore sheepskin coats and woolen hats and mittens. Their clothes generally smelled like wood smoke that probably masked other odors.

Sun Up, Sun Down (A Peasant's Life)

Sun up, sun down—in the shadow of the castle he stays.
Sun up, sun down—he's a peasant in medieval days.

(Peasant)
I work in the field with my sickle and spade
And cart the grain back to the mill.
I pay the lord's taxes then tend to my sheep,
And I suffer the cool, autumn chill.

Sun up, sun down—in the shadow of the castle he stays.
Sun up, sun down—he's a peasant in medieval days.

(Peasant)
My dark, one-room home's built of wattle and daub,
The roof made of reeds, tied and straight.
I look to my lord for protection from harm.
It's my life on the feudal estate.

Sun up, sun down—in the shadow of the castle he stays.
Sun up, sun down—he's a peasant in medieval days.
Sun up, sun down—he's a peasant in medieval days.

From *In the Middle of the Middle Ages: Integrating Content Standards and the Arts*. By Mary Wheeler and Jill Terlep. Music by Mary Wheeler. Illustrations by Jill Terlep. Westport, CT: Libraries Unlimited/Teacher Ideas Press. Copyright © 2007.

NAME _____ DATE_____

Sun Up, Sun Down (A Peasant's Life)

You are a peasant living in the medieval manorial system. It is a cool fall evening, and your work is done until early tomorrow morning. Compose a journal entry noting your day's activities. You can tell about your work, home, family, meals, clothing, feelings, or other things that happened today. Record at least one page, and be sure to write in complete sentences. Don't forget punctuation marks and capital letters, too.

Dear Journal,

_____
_____
_____
_____
_____
_____
_____
_____
_____
_____
_____
_____
_____
_____
_____
_____
_____
_____
_____
_____
_____

From In the Middle of the Middle Ages: Integrating Content Standards and the Arts. *By Mary Wheeler and Jill Terlep. Music by Mary Wheeler. Illustrations by Jill Terlep. Westport, CT: Libraries Unlimited/Teacher Ideas Press. Copyright © 2007.*

Sir Richard, Child to Knight

Setting the Stage

In a noble family, when the firstborn son reached the age of seven or eight years, he was sent to another wealthy household to begin his duties as a page. Serving the neighboring lord, the page ran errands, waited on knights and the noble families, and performed household services. Academic education began at this time, and the page's studies covered a variety of subjects: limited geography, some French or Latin, reading, writing, and religion. Social behaviors—deportment, manners, cleanliness, singing, dancing—were also taught. The code of chivalry and courtly love was stressed and very important in the training.

The page began learning the necessary skills for knighthood. He rode and cared for horses, and he practiced with bows and arrows. Even childhood games such as wrestling and playing tag built his physical strength. As he got older, he hunted and started training with weapons.

When he was about 13 or 14 years old, he became a squire and was apprenticed to a knight. The knight's job was to train him for warfare, honing all of the necessary skills. In return, the squire looked after his master's armor, helmet, and weapons. Among the youth's other duties were caring for the knight's horses and personal belongings. In later years, the squire was expected to follow his master onto the battlefield and attend to his needs.

The young man spent countless hours drilling on horseback with his lance. Riding toward a post with a straw-filled sack, representing a future enemy, the squire tried to hit the quintain in the middle with his lance. If he did not, the beam swung around and hit the boy in the back.

Hunting, hawking, weaponry, swordsmanship, archery, horsemanship, and all of the games of war were practiced. During the training, the squire wore armor to prepare himself for battles.

Knighthood could be granted in several ways. A king, before a battle, could name someone a knight to encourage loyalty and support. Another knight on a battlefield could bestow the title to a brave fighter. If there was time, the squire was dubbed in a religious ceremony. The night before the ritual, after bathing and donning a white linen tunic, the squire confessed his sins. Before the altar of the Church, following mass and communion the next day, the squire promised his faithfulness and loyalty to his lord and his king. With a tap of the blade of a sword on his shoulder, he was knighted.

Commoners—even peasants or serfs—as well as noblemen could become knights. If a man showed exceptional courage or heroism on the battlefield, it was not unusual for him to be rewarded with knighthood.

However, being a knight was expensive. Horses, armor, weapons, and tunics cost a lot of money. Also, household expenses had to be paid. Unless a man possessed land or money (or both), he could not afford the life of a knight.

Sir Richard, Child to Knight

He promised to be faithful and protect him with a sword,
And before the altar, vowed to serve the manor of his lord.
He studied hard, and finally, in a solemn feudal rite—
A nobleman, a vassal—he was dubbed a trusted knight.

When Richard was a little boy, he was called a page.
He became a squire next at fourteen years of age.
At last, he turned into a knight, and he was very proud.
He loved to say his name and said it many times aloud.

Sir Richard, Sir Richard, Sir Richard is my name.
Sir Richard, Sir Richard, Sir Richard is my name.
Sir Richard, Sir Richard, Sir Richard is my name.
Sir Richard, Sir Richard, Sir Richard is my name.

NAME _____ DATE _____

Sir Richard, Child to Knight

Pretend that you are young Richard as a page or a squire. Write a conversation that you have with your knight in training. You can discuss geography, chivalry, manners, warfare, armor, horses, hunting, family, or any other topic of interest to you. Use proper punctuation marks, and don't forget to indent each time you change speakers.

Pillory on the Village Green

Setting the Stage

Among the responsibilities of the feudal lord was the administering of justice. Seated at the high table in the great hall, the lord held court. If he was powerful, the lord could dispense severe punishments, such as branding; cutting off a thumb, hand, or ear; or even execution. Vassals or knights could settle lesser crimes.

Criminal actions varied from drunkenness to gambling, swearing, fighting, and wife beating. Poachers, pickpockets, cheating merchants, vagrants, petty thieves, and unruly servants also were penalized. The nobleman ruled on all cases in which castle regulations were broken. Such regulations might include failure to attend chapel, oversleeping, stealing, or embezzling food.

Punishments differed. A dispute over property, for example, might simply call for a decision, but other arguments required fines. More serious violations received even stiffer sentences, such as dunking the offenders in lakes or rivers, locking them in stocks or pillories, and imprisoning them in dungeons.

Pillories were placed in public areas like marketplaces, crossroads, or common areas, such as the village greens. The pillories were constructed of two hinged timbers, connected to two vertical, supporting beams. Standing, the violator placed his head and hands on the cutouts of the bottom board. The top timber was then lowered and locked. Once his head and hands were fixed in place, the offender could not move. Duration of time varied from one to two hours to a whole day.

Serving as a source of entertainment for the locals, the wrongdoers were taunted, jeered, and tormented by those who passed by. Rotten eggs or meat, filth, dead animal carcasses, and stones were hurled at the violators for further abuse.

From In the Middle of the Middle Ages: Integrating Content Standards and the Arts. *By Mary Wheeler and Jill Terlep. Music by Mary Wheeler. Illustrations by Jill Terlep. Westport, CT: Libraries Unlimited/Teacher Ideas Press. Copyright © 2007.*

Pillory on the Village Green

It was a crime I didn't mean,
And now each passerby has seen
My head and hands and legs between
These timbers on the village green.

I hid my face as I was led
To village green and sadly said,
"I nevermore will get ahead
By cheating; I'll be fair instead."

Oh, the pillory on the village green!

Ha! Ha! Ha! Hee! Hee! Hee! I know it isn't funny, but you see—
Ha! Ha! Ha! Hee! Hee! Hee! I'm laughing 'cause it tickles on my knee.

When my nose was twitching
I could use my hands for itching,
But my hands can't reach to scratch my knee.

Ha! Ha! Ha! Hee! Hee! Hee! I know it isn't funny, but you see—
Ha! Ha! Ha! Hee! Hee! Hee! I'm laughing 'cause it tickles on my knee.

Would you scratch that little tickle on my knee?

NAME _____ DATE _____

Pillory on the Village Green

List 10 violations for which you could be punished in the Middle Ages.

_____   _____
_____   _____
_____   _____
_____   _____
_____   _____

True or False?

1. _____ One of the feudal lord's jobs was to administer justice.

2. _____ Court was conducted at the marketplace.

3. _____ Only the king could order an execution.

4. _____ If a castle rule was broken, the violator could be punished.

5. _____ Punishments were the same for all offenses.

6. _____ Disputes over property required big fines.

7. _____ If a person committed a serious crime, he could be dunked in a lake.

8. _____ Stocks, pillories, and dungeons were used to confine criminals.

9. _____ Pillories were placed in wooded forests where the violators were hidden from view.

10. _____ The violator had to stand between two huge beams on the pillory.

11. _____ Local people often teased those who were confined to the pillory.

12. _____ The village green was a common area used by many people.

Castle in Motion

Setting the Stage

During the Middle Ages, many people thought monsters, such as dragons, lived in strange regions and guarded treasures in caves or shelters. They also believed in witches and wizards, who could cast magic spells.

Around 1130 AD, Geoffrey of Monmouth wrote the *History of the Kings of Britain,* and in his book he recounted the tales of King Arthur and his Round Table. How much of his stories were based on fact and how much on fiction is unknown, but the tales became very popular.

If Arthur did exist, he probably lived sometime between 400 and 600 AD, but it is unlikely that he had a Round Table and a group of knights in shining armor. Arthur may have been a famous warrior, or his life may have been based on more than one historical person.

Stories of his legendary deeds were retold for hundreds of years. During the 11th through 15th centuries, the tales were associated with love, bravery, chivalry, and a belief in magic. The values and ideals were reflections of the times.

Merlin the magician is one of the most interesting figures in Arthurian stories, but Geoffrey created Merlin's character. Merlin, known as Merlinus, first appeared around 1135. Depending on the story, Merlin was Arthur's advisor, his magician in the court of Camelot, his prophet, and more.

Whether fact or fiction, all of the Arthurian figures—King Arthur, Guinevere, Merlin, Sir Lancelot, and many others, as well as Excalibur and Camelot—have fascinated and entertained people from the Middle Ages to present times.

The walls, towers, moats, and drawbridges were architectural features of medieval castles. The earliest fortresses were built of earth and wood, but by the 1100s, most were constructed of stone. Walls could be several yards thick. Towers provided elevated locations for soldiers to watch the surrounding countryside for dangers. Moats and drawbridges served as outer defense barriers.

From In the Middle of the Middle Ages: Integrating Content Standards and the Arts. *By Mary Wheeler and Jill Terlep. Music by Mary Wheeler. Illustrations by Jill Terlep. Westport, CT: Libraries Unlimited/Teacher Ideas Press. Copyright © 2007.*

Castle in Motion

(Guinevere)
Merlin the magician lived in the days of knights
And kings and queens and dragons who were very frightful sights.
Chivalry was Merlin's code, but magic was his trade.
In castles of medieval times, his wondrous tricks were played.

King Arthur summoned Merlin one dark and stormy night.
Said,

(King Arthur)
"Royal feasting's made me fat. My armor's much too tight."

(Guinevere)
So Merlin picked some palace chores to play some music to.
He created Castle-Motions for King Arthur's Court to do.

(Merlin)
Swim a moat. Row a boat.
Round the table if you're able.
Climb the tower. You've got the power.
Ride a horse, again, of course.
Stretch your bow. Knead the dough.
Shoot an arrow, straight and narrow.
Push a plow. You know how.
Stir the brew, backwards, too.
Foe on ridge, draw the bridge.
Scale a wall. Do not fall.
Catch the dragon. Load the wagon.
Wave your sword like a lord.

(All, or Merlin alone)
Camelot was long ago. If Merlin lived today,
He would tell you,
"Listen close,"
And you would hear him say,
"Do the Castle-Motions to keep healthy and stay well.
Exercise is magic. You don't need a wizard's spell."

Do the Castle-Motions.

NAME _____ DATE_____

Castle in Motion

Choose an Arthurian character—King Arthur, Merlin, or Guinevere—and write a letter to that person. (Include the five parts of a friendly letter.) Tell why you would be a valuable member of the Round Table. Are you brave, courageous, or honorable? What about the code of chivalry? Do you have special skills that make you a good knight or lady? You can exaggerate like the stories of King Arthur do.

(Heading) _____

_____

_____ _(Greeting)_

(Body) _____

_____

_____

_____

_____

_____

_____

_____

_____

_____

_____

_____

_____

_____

_____

(Closing) _____

(Signature) _____

From _In the Middle of the Middle Ages: Integrating Content Standards and the Arts._ By Mary Wheeler and Jill Terlep. Music by Mary Wheeler. Illustrations by Jill Terlep. Westport, CT: Libraries Unlimited/Teacher Ideas Press. Copyright © 2007.

This Riddle

Setting the Stage

Growth of cities and increased trade encouraged the improvement of accounting skills. A tool known as the abacas was introduced in the West during the 10th century, and it was a faster way of calculating than "finger-reckoning." Roman numerals were still used, but they were impractical for solving arithmetic problems requiring multiplication and division. European mathematicians were ready for change.

Leonardo Pisano (1170–1250) was an Italian mathematician who introduced Arabic numerals and their place value system to Europe. A member of the Bonacci family, Leonardo was nicknamed Fibonacci. Today, his Fibonacci sequence, a number pattern, is used in various areas of math and science.

Fibonacci was born in Pisa, Italy, but his father, Guglielmo, served as a consul in North Africa. Because he represented the merchants of Pisa, his father understood accounting and recognized the value of using the Arabic number system. It was in Bugia (Bejaia, Algeria) where he had Leonardo educated in mathematics.

The symbols were really developed in India around 400 BC by the Hindus. Arabs adopted and spread them to other cultures.

Fibonacci realized Arabic numerals were easier to use than Roman numerals for calculating. He traveled to several countries studying arithmetic.

Liber Abaci (Book of Calculations) was written by Fibonacci and published in 1202. The book introduced the "Indian" numeral system to Europe, and it showed the importance of using the symbols (1–9) in accounting, measuring, and other applications. Leonardo considered the numeral 0 a sign, and he did not recognize zero as a number. His hand-copied books received widespread interest and acceptance.

With the invention of the printing press in 1450, many people learned the number system. By the 16th century, Europeans commonly used Arabic numerals.

I Reckon

I "reckoned" with my fingers, but it wasn't very fast.
These numerals are better. I can multiply at last.
With symbols, one through nine, to work, our future has been cast.
We'll use them for accounting; finger "reckoning" is passed.

Clue

Take a trip so you can learn.
Hungry Herald should return
After symbols; it's okay.
Rumble, grumble goes away.

From *In the Middle of the Middle Ages: Integrating Content Standards and the Arts.* By Mary Wheeler and Jill Terlep. Music by Mary Wheeler. Illustrations by Jill Terlep. Westport, CT: Libraries Unlimited/Teacher Ideas Press. Copyright © 2007.

This Riddle

This riddle is confusing,
And my brain I know I'm using,
But I need to solve this riddle right away.
This riddle's not amusing,
And it's minutes we are losing
'Cause poor Herald needs some food and yet today!

I'm thinking! I'm thinking! I'll get it I know.
To help Hungry Herald I'll search high and low.
I'm sure I will figure the answer, although
This riddle's not easy to solve, so, let's go!

In the play, *In the Middle of the Middle Ages*, a dragon named Herald is hungry and needs more bread. He uses the *Clue* to find an answer to *This Riddle*.

Answer to *This Riddle*—

Arabic symbols (1, 2, 3, 4, 5, 6, 7, 8, 9 and the sign 0) and their place value system help Herald learn how to count his loaves of bread so that he has enough.

NAME _____ DATE_____

This Riddle

Who? What? When? Where?
(Answer in complete sentences.)

1. When was the abacas introduced to the West?
   _____

2. What are two reasons for the need for improved accounting skills?
   _____

3. When was Leonardo Pisano born?
   _____

4. Where was Fibonacci (Leonardo) born?
   _____

5. What was Fibonacci's father's job?
   _____

6. Whom did Guglielmo represent in his work?
   _____

7. What subject did Fibonacci study in several countries?
   _____

8. When was Fibonacci's book *Liber Abaci* published?
   _____

9. Where were the Arabic symbols really developed?
   _____

10. What invention hastened the adoption of the Arabic numerals?
    _____

From In the Middle of the Middle Ages: Integrating Content Standards and the Arts. *By Mary Wheeler and Jill Terlep. Music by Mary Wheeler.*
Illustrations by Jill Terlep. Westport, CT: Libraries Unlimited/Teacher Ideas Press. Copyright © 2007.

Let's compare number systems.

Roman Numeral values: I = 1   V = 5   X = 10

Using those symbols, solve the following problem: VIII + XXIII

Explain how you got your answer.

_____
_____
_____
_____
_____
_____
_____
_____
_____

Arabic Numerals:

Now add these numbers: 8
                         +23

Why is the Arabic number system much simpler to use?

_____
_____
_____
_____
_____
_____
_____
_____

What are the next three numbers in the pattern?
   (It's Fibonacci's number sequence.)

   1, 1, 2, 3, 5, 8, 13, _____, _____, _____

Two Cows

Setting the Stage

Girls were married at an early age, often at 12 to 14 years old. Betrothal of heiresses was sometimes made even before the age of five. Women frequently had several children by their 20s.

Marriages were not left to chance, and partners were chosen for reasons to help families build their defenses and finances. The ceremony was not only an agreement between two individuals, but also the bonding of two families.

All classes of people, but especially the upper classes, participated in arranged weddings. Love was not a consideration in an arranged marriage. Sometimes the marriage partners did develop affections for one another, but other times they lived together unhappily or in indifferent unions. Parents or guardians had the right to select whomever they wanted as husbands for their daughters or wards, but consent was required before the ceremony took place.

To the marriage, a bride brought a dowry, and she received from the groom a dower, about a third of the estate. Families discussed and agreed on the dowry the woman offered. It was considered a gift but often served as enticement to the man to accept the bride.

Depending on the wealth of the families involved, terms and conditions of the dowries varied. Peasants' dowries might consist of only a piece of furniture, but villagers with land might offer a portion of it and livestock, such as cows and pigs. Wealthy noble families provided fiefs, money, and other possessions.

After the wedding, the husband took charge of the household, even if the wife initially provided the land. With the marriage, the woman's economic rights ended.

If the bride and groom agreed that they wanted to marry, their consent created the bond. The wedding ceremony could take place anywhere—in a home, tavern, outdoors, or in a church.

The church was, however, the most popular location for weddings. Marital rituals occurred outside the church doors, and the nuptial mass took place inside. Many of the wedding traditions of today, such as the ceremonial positions of the bride and groom, exchanges of rings, and spoken vows, originated in the Middle Ages.

Two Cows

I have one hundred sheep, and a boar, seven sows,
And three big draught horses to pull my two plows.
I bring to this marriage the rent from my land
Of forty-two shillings, along with my hand.
The dowry's been offered, and I am a ward.
My husband and the wedding were arranged by the lord.

I own two cows. I guess they go, too.
Will I be happy? I wish they knew.
I own two cows. I guess they go, too.
Will I be happy? I wish they knew.

I wish I knew.

From *In the Middle of the Middle Ages: Integrating Content Standards and the Arts.* By Mary Wheeler and Jill Terlep. Music by Mary Wheeler. Illustrations by Jill Terlep. Westport, CT: Libraries Unlimited/Teacher Ideas Press. Copyright © 2007.

NAME _____ DATE_____

Two Cows

Write a paragraph about …

why you believe dowries worked for families in the Middle Ages.

_____
_____
_____
_____

why you believe dowries won't work for families in the present time.

_____
_____
_____
_____

Draw a picture of a bride in the Middle Ages with her dowry. She can be from any of the classes in the manorial system. Her marriage was arranged. Include the groom or other family members if you wish. You might choose to illustrate the poem *Two Cows* or show the bride with a new list of items that you selected.

From In the Middle of the Middle Ages: Integrating Content Standards and the Arts. By Mary Wheeler and Jill Terlep. Music by Mary Wheeler. Illustrations by Jill Terlep. Westport, CT: Libraries Unlimited/Teacher Ideas Press. Copyright © 2007.

Castle Terms—Vocabulary

Some castle terms to know:

bailey—a courtyard and surrounding walls

bakery—a place where goods were baked

battlements—patterned, defensive shields of stone, atop castle walls

chambers—enclosed spaces, personal quarters of the lord and lady

chapel—a place for worship in the residence

drawbridge—a movable bridge, raised to prevent intruders from entering

dungeon—an area where prisoners were kept, often located beneath the gatehouse tower

farm—land near the castle, worked by peasants and owned by the lord

garden—a space reserved for growing herbs, fruits, flowers, vegetables, and plants

garderobe—toilet area, often with wooden seats

gatehouse—a structure, usually consisting of two towers, located at a castle's entryway and intended to control traffic

great hall—a large room for eating meals, entertaining guests, and administering business

keep—the largest or central building of a castle, the main residence

kitchen—a place where food was prepared

loophole—a slit or loop in the castle wall that allowed weapons to be fired from the castle grounds

mill—a place with equipment to grind grain for flour

moat—a protective water-filled ditch, which surrounded the outside of the castle

motte—a mound of soil, several feet high, on which early castles were built

orchard—an area for planting fruit trees

portcullis—an open-patterned, grill gate at a castle's entry, behind the drawbridge, used as an extra barrier

stable—a building with stalls for sheltering animals, especially horses

storeroom—a room where goods were stored

tower—a high lookout structure, located in a strategic, defensive place

walkway—located atop the castle wall, a place for the sentry to maintain watch

walls—barriers several yards thick, made of layers, surrounding the castle

well—a drinking-water source

If the castle was large enough, it included other features such as a pond, a laundry, a brew house, an armory, a smithy, and kennels.

The settlement or village near the castle was under its protection. In return, the peasants or serfs farmed the surrounding land that belonged to the lord. Typically, the village included houses, a church, a mill, and the village green.

NAME _____ DATE _____

Castle Terms Crossword Puzzle

walkway	mill	great hall	walls
stable	bailey	battlements	garderobe
tower	moat	gatehouse	well
farm	garden	storeroom	portcullis
orchard			

ACROSS
3. patterned, defensive shields of stone
5. high lookout structure
8. open-patterned grill gate at castle's entry
9. land near castle, worked by peasants
10. atop castle wall, sentry watch
12. toilet area
14. surrounded castle
15. structure at castle entryway
16. building with stalls for sheltering animals

DOWN
1. courtyard and surrounding walls
2. room where goods were stored
4. large room for eating meals
6. area for planting fruit trees
7. place with equipment to grind grain
11. space reserved for growing plants
13. protective water-filled ditch
14. drinking-water source

NAME _____ DATE_____

Castle in Progress

Plan your own castle. Make a three-dimensional drawing; show it from the top (a bird's-eye view), or draw a profile (side view). Include some of the features in the *Castle Terms—Vocabulary* list. Add your own ideas or improvements, too. Make it a safe fortress. You can even add people at work or play.

Medieval Terms—Vocabulary

Some words to know:

armor (armour)—defensive clothing, often made of metal, worn to protect the body from weapons

baron—the most powerful and wealthy nobleman, received fief directly from the king

bishop—a powerful member of the Church who ruled over priests and monasteries

castle—a fortress, usually included several structures, surrounded by protective walls

cathedral—a large, important church

chivalry—a code of rules that reflected values and ideals, such as bravery and honor

Christian—a person who believes in Jesus Christ and lives according to his teachings

concentric circles—circles sharing the same center

conqueror—one who wins by using force

crossbow—a bow-and-arrow weapon with the bow situated crosswise on wood

Crusades—military expeditions undertaken by Christians, lasting more than 200 years, aimed at recapturing the Holy Land from Muslim control

dowry—a gift, often property, given to the groom by the bride in marriage

famine—a severe food shortage covering a wide area

fealty—faithfulness and loyalty pledged to a lord by his vassal

feudalism—the political and economic system of the Middle Ages in which a vassal received land (fief) from a lord in exchange for service and protection; a pyramid of power with the king at the top and peasants or serfs at the base

fief—a parcel of land in the feudal system

halberd—a medieval weapon with an axe-like blade on a wooden shaft

illumination—a detailed, ornamental drawing that decorated a manuscript

joust—a tournament fighting match between two knights

lance—a knight's weapon that was a long wooden pole with a sharp point

knight—a medieval, mounted warrior who gave military service to a superior

lady—a feminine title of nobility

lord—one who held rank over another and from whom the feudal fee or estate was received, masculine title of nobility

Magna Carta—a document signed by King John, 1215, and the basis of the modern English Constitution

manor—a lord's domain in the feudal system

manorial system—based on agriculture, a system of land management where land was divided into manors

medieval—pertaining to the Middle Ages

merchant—one who sells goods for profit

monastery—a place where religious people live and work

minstrel—a medieval musical entertainer

Muslim—an adherent of Islam who believes in the teachings of Muhammad

nobility—upper class of people, gained by birth or rank, such as a duke or a king

page—a boy in first stage of training for knighthood, around ages 7 through 14 years

peasant—a member of the lowest class who farmed the land for a lord

plague—an infectious disease affecting large numbers of people

pillory—wooden framework with holes for head and hands, used to punish and confine violators or criminals

poacher—a person who fishes or hunts on another's property

Roman Empire—lands ruled by Rome, starting about 27 BC, declining in the late fourth century, and ending AD 476

sentry—a guard

serf—a servant bound to the soil

shield—a protective metal armor used by the knight during battle

squire—an attendant to the knight and ranked just below him in the feudal system

tournaments—contests between knights

vassal—a person who held land (fief) from a feudal lord in return for fealty or loyalty

village green—the commons area in a town or village, grassy land

wattle and daub—construction materials for peasants' homes; wattle is interwoven twigs and sticks; daub is clay mixed with straw

From In the Middle of the Middle Ages: Integrating Content Standards and the Arts. *By Mary Wheeler and Jill Terlep. Music by Mary Wheeler. Illustrations by Jill Terlep. Westport, CT: Libraries Unlimited/Teacher Ideas Press. Copyright © 2007.*

NAME _____ DATE _____

Medieval Terms Crossword Puzzle

tournament	baron	page	lady
bishop	peasant	illumination	crossbow
chivalry	famine	poacher	joust
merchant	dowry	manorial system	lord
halberd	squire	lance	

ACROSS
1. severe food shortage
3. detailed ornamental drawing
6. one who held rank over another
8. code of rules
11. powerful member of the church
14. boy at first stage of training for knighthood
16. tournament fighting match
17. one of the most powerful noble titles
18. contest between knights

DOWN
2. system of land management
4. feminine title of nobility
5. one who sells good for profit
6. wooden pole weapon
7. weapon with axe-like blade
9. weapon with bow
10. member of the lowest class
12. attendant to a knight
13. person who hunts on another's property
15. gift given to a groom

A Story for the Ages (Middle)

Choose at least 10 words from the *Medieval Terms—Vocabulary* list. Write a story. Underline the words you chose from the list. When you finish, practice reading it to yourself. Be ready to share it with others.

Medieval Figures—Vocabulary

Some people to know:

(lifespans are approximate)

Alaric—(370–410) Visigoth tribal chieftain, lead the march on Rome in 410

Alfred the Great—(849–899) first sovereign ruler of England, led from 871 to 899; known as great warrior and a social reformer

Roger Bacon—(1214–1292) scholar and scientist, promoted scientific method

Thomas Becket—(1118–1170) advisor to Henry II, became archbishop and later canonized

Geoffrey Chaucer—(1340–1400) poet, author of *Canterbury Tales*

Simon de Montfort—(1207–1265) led opposition against Henry III because he thought the king was a poor leader

Duke of Normandy—(1028–1087) known as William the Conqueror, led the Norman invasion of England in 1066; reigned as king from 1066 to 1087

Geoffrey of Monmouth—(1100–1155) author of *History of the Kings of Britain,* the popular book about King Arthur and the Round Table

**Johann Gutenberg**—(1398–1468) known for inventing the printing press

Henry—(1068–1135) king of England from 1100 to 1135; son of William the Conqueror

Henry II—(1133–1189) king of England from 1154 to 1189; founded Plantagenet royal line; his knights murdered archbishop Thomas Becket in 1170; grandson of Henry I

Henry III—(1207–1272) king of England from 1216 to 1272; succeeded his father, King John; opposed by Simon de Montfort

John of England—(1167–1216) king of England from 1199 to 1216; forced to sign the Magna Carta

Genghis Khan (Chinggis Kahn)—(1138–1227) conqueror and fierce leader of the Mongols

King Arthur—legendary king, said to have led the Knights of the Round Table; probably a myth

Merlin—magician and prophet who served King Arthur in Arthurian legends

Muhammad—(570–632) Prophet of Islam

Pope Urban II—(1042–1099) urged Christians to retake the Holy Lands in his speech in 1095; initiated the Crusades

Queen Isabella—(1452–1504) queen of Spain, sponsored Christopher Columbus's voyage to America in 1492

Richard the Lion-Hearted—(1157–1199) king of England from 1189 to 1199; known as a mighty warrior

St. Francis—(1181–1226) known as St. Francis of Assisi, canonized within two years of his death; founder of the Franciscan Order of priests

John Wyclif—(1330–1384) church reformer and forerunner of Protestant Reformation

NAME _____ DATE _____

Middle Ages Figures Crossword

Thomas Becket	Duke of Normandy	Johann Gutenberg
Alaric	Merlin	Alfred the Great
Henry	King Arthur	Geoffrey Chaucer
Roger Bacon		

ACROSS
5. first sovereign ruler of England
6. prophet who served King Arthur
8. name of three kings of England
9. advisor to Henry II, canonized
10. William the Conqueror

DOWN
1. author of *Canterbury Tales*
2. promoted scientific method
3. legendary king of the Roundtable
4. invented printing press
7. Visigoth tribal chieftain

NAME _____ DATE _____

Medieval Figures—A Biography

Choose a figure from the Middle Ages. It can be someone listed in the *Medieval Figures—Vocabulary* list, or you can select another person from that time with your instructor's approval. Read a biography about that person.

Person chosen: _____

Title: _____

Author: _____

Why was this person important or famous?

_____

_____

_____

_____

What did this figure accomplish or attempt?

_____

_____

_____

Write three questions that you would have liked to ask this person.

1. _____

2. _____

3. _____

How were other people's lives changed because of this biographical subject?

_____

_____

_____

Write a one-page summary of the book.

From In the Middle of the Middle Ages: Integrating Content Standards and the Arts. *By Mary Wheeler and Jill Terlep. Music by Mary Wheeler. Illustrations by Jill Terlep. Westport, CT: Libraries Unlimited/Teacher Ideas Press. Copyright © 2007.*

NAME _____ DATE _____

Middle Ages Figures

Subtract each problem. Match the answer with the years of each of the Middle Ages characters. Write the letter of your answer and the life span in years. With many people, years are approximate because centuries-old records aren't exact.

A. 1468 −1398	B. 1226 −1181	C. 1087 −1028	D. 899 −849
E. 1155 −1100	F. 1099 −1042	G. 1384 −1330	H. 1292 −1214
I. 1227 −1138	J. 1170 −1118 52	K. 1504 −1451	L. 632 −570
M. 1216 −1167	N. 1400 −1340	O. 1265 −1207	P. 410 −370

1. Sir Thomas Becket   52 years.   _J_   (1118–1170)
2. Johann Gutenberg   70 years.   ___   (_____)
3. Roger Bacon   78 years.   ___   (_____)
4. Alaric   40 years.   ___   (_____)
5. Geoffrey Chaucer   60 years.   ___   (_____)
6. St. Francis   45 years.   ___   (_____)
7. Genghis Khan   89 years.   ___   (_____)
8. John of England   49 years.   ___   (_____)
9. Muhammad   62 years.   ___   (_____)
10. William the Conqueror 59 years. ___   (_____)
11. Pope Urban II   57 years.   ___   (_____)
12. John Wyclif   54 years.   ___   (_____)
13. Geoffrey of Monmouth 55 years. ___   (_____)
14. Queen Isabella   53 years.   ___   (_____)
15. Simon de Montfort   58 years.   ___   (_____)
16. Alfred the Great   50 years.   ___   (_____)

Bonus: What was the average life span of these people? _____

From In the Middle of the Middle Ages: Integrating Content Standards and the Arts. By Mary Wheeler and Jill Terlep. Music by Mary Wheeler. Illustrations by Jill Terlep. Westport, CT: Libraries Unlimited/Teacher Ideas Press. Copyright © 2007.

Setting the Stage Additional Reading List

Students might require more information to complete an assignment, or they might exhibit curiosity about one of the topics. Here is a list of books that go beyond the *Setting the Stage* background information pages. Some of the books in this section are nonfiction—for example, the books on the art of illumination. Other books in this list are fiction, such as those retelling the legend of King Arthur and those about medieval minstrels.

Following the play is an *Additional Reading List*. These books apply to *Research and Discovery Activities* and other aspects of medieval life. Some of the titles on the list will be found there as well.

Illuminations

Note: The following books on the art of illumination are all found in the adult section of your library or bookseller. Please review content to ensure that it is appropriate for your students.

Grafton, Belanger Carol. *Illuminated Initials in Full Color: 548 Designs.* New York: Dover, 1995.

Jones, Owen. *1001 Illuminated Initial Letters: 27 Full-Color Plates.* New York: Dover, 1988.

Lovett, Patricia. *Calligraphy & Illumination: A History and Practical Guide.* New York: Harry N. Abrams, 2005.

Shaw, Henry, ed. *Medieval Alphabets and Decorative Devices.* New York: Dover, 1999.

Thomson, George. *The Illuminated Lettering Kit: Materials, Techniques, and Projects for Decorative Calligraphy.* Chronicle Books, 2004.

Traveling Minstrel

Avi. *Crispin: The Cross of Lead.* New York: Hyperion Books for Children, 2002.

Haahr, Berit I. *Minstrel's Tale.* New York: Delacorte Press, 2000.

Sutcliff, Rosemary. *Minstrel and the Dragon Pup.* First American ed. Boston: Candlewick Press, 1993.

Salted Meats and Pickled Beets

Aliki. *A Medieval Feast.* New York: Crowell, 1983.

Dawson, Imogen. *Food & Feasts in the Middle Ages*. New York: New Discovery Books, 1994.

Elliott, Lynne. *Food and Feasts in the Middle Ages*. New York: Crabtree Pub. Co., 2004.

Marching to the Crusades

Cadnum, Michael. *The Book of the Lion*. New York: Viking, 2000.

Crossley-Holland, Kevin. *King of the Middle March*. First American ed. New York: Arthur A. Levine, 2004.

Daly-Weir, Catherine. *Coat of Arms*. New York: Grosset & Dunlap, 2000.

Doherty, Katherine M., and Craig A. Doherty. *King Richard the Lionhearted and the Crusades in World History*. Berkeley Heights, NJ: Enslow, 2002.

Grant, K. M. *Blood Red Horse*. New York: Walker, 2005.

Madden, Thomas. *Crusades: The Illustrated History*. Ann Arbor: University of Michigan Press, 2004.

Riley-Smith, Jonathan. *The Atlas of the Crusades*. New York: Facts on File, 1991.

Riley-Smith, Jonathan, ed. *The Oxford History of the Crusades*. Oxford and New York: Oxford University Press, 1999.

Sun Up, Sun Down

Beckett, Sister Wendy. *The Duke and the Peasant: Life in the Middle Ages: Adventures in Art Series*. New York: Prestel, 1997.

Eastwood, Kay. *Medieval Society*. New York: Crabtree, 2003.

Padrino, Mercedes. *Feudalism and Village Life in the Middle Ages*. Milwaukee: World Almanac Library, 2006.

Sir Richard, Child to Knight

Gibbons, Gail. *Knights in Shining Armor*. Boston: Little Brown, 1995.

Gravett, Christopher. *Knight: Eyewitness Books*. New York: Dorling Kindersley, 2000.

McGovern, Ann. *If You Lived in the Days of Knights*. New York: Scholastic, 2001.

Platt, Richard. *Castle Diary: The Journal of Tobias Burgess, Page.* Cambridge, MA: Candlewick Press, 1999.

Reid, Struan. *Lift the Lid on Knights: Explore a Medieval World of Chivalry and Adventure and Build Your Own Knight.* Philadelphia: Running Press, 2001.

Walker, Jane. *100 Things You Should Know about Knights & Castles.* Broomall, PA: Mason Crest, 2003.

Weatherly, Myra. *William Marshall: Medieval England's Greatest Knight.* Greensboro, NC: Morgan Reynolds, 2001.

Pillory on the Village Green

MacDonald, Fiona. *You Wouldn't Want to Be in a Medieval Dungeon!: Prisoners You'd Rather Not Meet.* New York: Franklin Watts, 2003.

Trembinski, Donna. *Law and Punishment in the Middle Ages.* New York: Crabtree, 2006.

Castle in Motion

Crossley-Holland, Kevin. *At the Crossing-Places.* First American ed. New York: Arthur A. Levine, 2002.

Crossley-Holland, Kevin. *The Seeing Stone.* First American ed. New York: Arthur A. Levine, 2001.

Gravett, Christopher. *Eyewitness: Castle* (Eyewitness Books). Rev. ed. New York: DK, 2004.

Hodges, Margaret, reteller. *Merlin and the Making of the King.* New York: Holiday House, 2004.

Morris, Gerald. *The Squire's Tale.* Boston: Houghton Mifflin, 1998.

Pyle, Howard, adapted by Joshua Hanft. *King Arthur and the Knights of the Round Table.* Edina, MN: Abdo, 2002.

Reid, Struan. *Castle Life.* Austin, TX: Raintree Steck-Vaughn, 1999.

San Souci, Robert D. *Young Arthur.* New York: Doubleday Books for Young Readers, 1997.

San Souci, Robert D. *Young Guinevere.* New York: Doubleday, 1993.

San Souci, Robert D. *Young Merlin*. New York: Doubleday, 1990.

Steele, Philip. *The World of Castles*. Boston: Kingfisher, a Houghton Mifflin Company Imprint, 2005.

Yolen, Jane. *Sword of the Rightful King: A Novel of King Arthur*. San Diego: Harcourt, 2003.

This Riddle

Hulme, Joy N. *Wild Fibonacci: Nature's Secret Code Revealed!* Berkeley: Tricycle Press, 2005.

Two Cows

Cushman, Karen. *Catherine, Called Birdy*. New York: HarperCollins Children's Books, 1995.

General Books on Medieval Life

Most of these titles cover the topics of knights, castle life, feudalism, feasts, peasant life, weaponry, minstrels, and much more.

Adams, Simon. *Castles & Forts*. Boston: Kingfisher, a Houghton Mifflin Company Imprint, 2003.

Cole, Joanna. *Ms. Frizzle's Adventures: Medieval Castle*. New York: Scholastic, 2003.

Howarth, Sarah. *What Do We Know about the Middle Ages?* New York: Peter Bedrick Books, 1998.

Langley, Andrew. *Eyewitness Medieval Life,* rev. ed. New York: DK, 2004.

Leone, Bruno, ed. *The Middle Ages,* History Firsthand series. San Diego: Greenhaven Press, 2002.

MacDonald, Fiona. *Knights, Castles, and Warfare in the Middle Ages*. Milwaukee, WI: World Almanac Library, 2006.

Murrell, Deborah. *The Best Book of Knights and Castles*. Boston: Kingfisher, A Houghton Mifflin Company Imprint, 2005.

Rice, Earle, Jr. *Life During the Middle Ages,* Way People Live Series. San Diego: Lucent Books, 1998.

This is a great opportunity to work with your librarian to create your own reading list or even create a library display to encourage others to learn about the Middle Ages.

Research and Discovery Activities

NAME _____ DATE _____

Who's Who around the Table

Geoffrey of Monmouth wrote of King Arthur and other colorful characters in the 12th century. The book *History of the Kings of Britain* became very popular.

Retold and recreated by different storytellers and authors over the centuries, the characters' roles have changed. Lancelot, for example, varies from being the greatest of King Arthur's knights to the worst, a close friend to source of trouble. Gawain is portrayed as both. Other figures disappear and return. But with their tales of chivalry, romance, spiritualism, and heroism, even today the legends continue to fascinate and entertain audiences.

King Arthur	Sir Bedivere	Sir Gawain	Sir Kay
Merlin	Sir Galahad	Guinevere	Sir Lancelot
Camelot	Excalibur	Round Table	Holy Grail

Let's continue the legend. Choose from the Arthurian members and terms above, or add your own. Maybe you already have some favorite characters that you want to include. Write your tale of King Arthur and his Knights of the Round Table.

Remember that a good story needs the following things: a **setting,** the time and place of a story; **characters,** the people or creatures; and a **plot.** The plot includes a beginning, where a problem is presented. The middle of the plot tells what happens to develop the story, and the end tells how the problem is solved.

Adding dialogue or conversation can often make the narrative more interesting. Also, the first sentence hooks your audience, so write a great one. An exciting or appealing title grabs attention, too.

Punctuation marks are the traffic signs for stories; without them readers can get lost or miss the message. Good tales dont't just happen!

Notes: _____

_____

_____

_____

_____

_____

_____

_____

_____

Planning the Story about King Arthur

Title:
_____

Beginning:
_____
_____

Middle:
_____
_____
_____
_____

End:
_____
_____
_____

Dialogue sample:
_____
_____
_____
_____

Opening sentence:
_____
_____
_____
_____

Write a rough draft. Make sure you edit, revise, and then proofread your final copy.

NAME _____ DATE_____

Books Change History

Johann Gutenberg (1398–1468) was born to a wealthy family in Mainz, Germany. Like his parents, Johann was a goldsmith. Around 1450, he developed one of the most important inventions in history, the printing press. If it had not been invented, the Industrial Revolution, as well as the cultural revolution of the Renaissance, would not have taken place.

The Chinese had already created movable, wooden type, but it wore down easily and lacked uniformity. Using an alloy of lead, tin, and antimony, Johann cast letters of metal. The system worked well, and between 1450 and 1455, the Gutenberg Bible was printed in Latin. Twenty-two copies are known to exist today, including one in the Library of Congress and two in European libraries.

Gutenberg died in poverty. However, he is recognized and credited for producing the machine that changed the history of the world.

Your assignment:

Johann Gutenberg walks into a mega-bookstore of the 21st century. His eyes are filled with wonder as he gazes at the vast display of printed materials. What questions does he ask?

_____
_____
_____
_____
_____
_____
_____
_____
_____
_____
_____

Here are ten other inventions from the Middle Ages. Rank them in order of their importance. Be prepared to explain your choices:

*buttons, paper, horseshoes, magnetic compass, eyeglasses,
gunpowder, underwear, forks, clocks, musical notes*

1. _____   6. _____
2. _____   7. _____
3. _____   8. _____
4. _____   9. _____
5. _____   10. _____

Perpetual Lamps and Flying Machines

Devoting his life to the pursuit of knowledge, Roger Bacon was a scholar and a scientist. He was one of the first people to use the modern scientific method of learning. Experimentation and observation, combined with mathematics and physics, enabled him to make discoveries and inventions far beyond the information of the times.

After teaching at both Oxford and the University of Paris, he joined the Franciscan Order as a friar in the early 1250s. Using the library of the convent, he learned Greek so he could read the texts of Aristotle. Bacon studied many subjects including alchemy, languages, astronomy, mathematics, physics, optics, and philosophy.

In the 1260s, Roger Bacon wrote the *Opus Majus* (Major Work). It was an encyclopedia of the sciences, identifying seven areas: optics, astronomy, weights, alchemy, biology, medicine, and experimental research. Pope Clement IV, who had requested the book, died in 1268, and Bacon's intended educational reforms were not realized. Two other books, *Opus Minus* and *Opus Tertium,* completed the three-volume set. Among other ideas, he wanted the sciences to have more prominent roles at the universities and for the Church to realize the sciences' importance. He was later imprisoned by the Church for heresy but was freed after several years.

Bacon's inventions, discoveries, and scientific predictions were decades or even centuries ahead of his time. He described or wrote of perpetual lamps, flying machines, diving apparatus, mechanical ships and carriages, submarines, and pulley systems. He believed one could sail around the Earth because it was a sphere. Studying optics, light refraction, and magnification, he proposed microscopes, lenses to aid vision, and telescopes to observe the sun, moon, and stars.

Most important, he laid the foundation for modern science. He promoted the scientific method and believed that mathematics was the key to its findings.

Your Assignment

Select a scientific project to explore. It can be any subject or area that interests you. Be accurate and follow careful guidelines as you study and learn, just like Roger Bacon. Investigate, demonstrate, test, research, or collect. Record and report your results. Include the five steps of the **scientific method:** state the problem, make observations, form a hypothesis, do the experiment, and draw a conclusion.

Notes: _____

Scientific Project

Problem:
_____
_____
_____
_____
_____

Observations:
_____
_____
_____
_____
_____

Hypothesis:
_____
_____
_____
_____

Experiment:
_____
_____
_____
_____

Conclusion:
_____
_____
_____
_____

NAME _____ DATE_____

Choose Your Weapons

Lord Marksman has received word that his manor will soon be attacked. He checks his arsenal and realizes that several weapons are needed. He quickly goes to his computer (Never mind how he got it!) and places an order on the Internet for the following items:

7 halberds (@$15.98)
9 lances (@$19.95)
10 shields, personalized with coat of arms (@$29.95)
11 crossbows (@$21.05)
5 axes (@$17.49)
Half box arrows, steel-tipped, (@$52.38 box, 144 in a box)

Internet address *(you name it)*: www._____.com

Credit Parchment # 10-14-1066, expires __ / __ __

Total the items in your shopping cart, and add $15.95 for overnight chariot delivery. Show all of your work.

Total amount _____

By the way, how did Lord Marksman get his computer?

_____

_____

From *In the Middle of the Middle Ages: Integrating Content Standards and the Arts.* By Mary Wheeler and Jill Terlep. Music by Mary Wheeler. Illustrations by Jill Terlep. Westport, CT: Libraries Unlimited/Teacher Ideas Press. Copyright © 2007.

NAME _____ DATE_____

Water, Water, Everywhere

The site of a village in the Middle Ages had to be located near water for several reasons. Of course, people needed water to drink. Water was also used to run waterwheels for mills, for irrigation to grow food, for transportation, and in trade.

No longer under the protection of the Roman Empire, two families have set out to find a new place to live. After passing by a wooded forest, they arrive at a river.

Using some or all of the reasons above, write a **two-person play,** between Henry and Leon, discussing why this is the spot to start their homes. You may need to add another page.

Henry: _____

_____

Leon: _____

_____

Henry: _____

_____

Leon: _____

_____

Henry: _____

_____

Leon: _____

_____

Henry: _____

_____

Leon: _____

_____

Henry: _____

_____

NAME _____ DATE _____

It's Time

Create a timeline.
Put the following eight events in order on the timeline. Include the year (or approximate year) that it occurred. Try using different colors.

Norman Invasion	Eighth Crusade
First Crusade	Johann Gutenberg invents printing press
Geoffrey of Monmouth writes *History of the Kings of Britain*	Fibonacci publishes *Liber Abaci*
Reign of Richard the Lionhearted	
King John signs *Magna Carta*	

Now, find five more events that occurred during the Middle Ages, different from those above. Locate their positions on this timeline. Which event would you have liked to participate in or watch? Why? (Put your answer on a separate sheet of paper.)

NAME _____ DATE _____

Johann Gutenberg Was the Best Inventor

A **fact** is something that can be proved true or false. An **opinion** tells a person's ideas or feelings. It cannot be proved true or false. Read these statements about Johann Gutenberg. Write fact or opinion.

Johann Gutenberg ...

1. was the best inventor of all time. _____

2. was born in the city of Mainz in Germany. _____

3. enjoyed inventing new machines. _____

4. was born to a wealthy patrician family of goldsmiths. _____

5. was excited when he sold copies of a two-volume Bible. _____

6. used metal type to form a mold for printing. _____

7. wanted to print a lot more books because he thought people would read them. _____

8. was a German metal worker. _____

9. needed more books to read so he started looking for a better way to make them. _____

10. sold copies of the Bible in 1455 for 300 florins each. _____

11. would be proud of his legacy today and how his invention has affected history. _____

12. did not include page numbers and paragraph breaks in his Gutenberg Bible. _____

13. was disappointed when he couldn't repay a loan to a partner in 1436. _____

Write a fact about yourself. _____

Write an opinion about yourself. _____

NAME _____ DATE_____

Plague or Famine?

During the 14th century, two great natural disasters occurred: the Great Famine and the Black Death. Together, they were the cause of millions—not thousands, but **millions**—of deaths. Choose either topic and write a research report.

In your report, cite at least three sources of information, and include at least one book among them. You may get facts from a dictionary, an encyclopedia, an almanac, an atlas, periodicals, the Internet, and other books.

Take notes so you will remember details, and write key words about what you want to tell in your report. Make sure that you do not copy sentences word for word.

An outline, where you write topics and subtopics, will help you organize your thoughts. From your outline, you can develop paragraphs. Use the main ideas in the outline to write your topic sentences, and let the subtopics provide the supporting facts.

Questions to consider if you choose to write about the—

Great Famine:

    What is a famine?

    How long did it last?

    When did it happen, and how many people lost their lives?

    What countries or areas were affected?

    What climate changes occurred to affect the growing of crops?

    What did people do to attempt to ward off hunger?

    How did population patterns of the age contribute to the famine?

    What were some of the consequences of the catastrophe?

Black Death:

    What is the Black Death, and what is another name for the disease?

    When did it occur, and how many people lost their lives?

    By what means was it spread?

    Where did it originate, and through which areas did it travel?

    How did the population patterns of the times contribute to the spread?

    What were the people's reactions?

    What kinds of preventative measures did the population take?

    How was it treated?

    What are ways to describe the devastation of families and villages?

    What were some of the consequences of the catastrophe?

From *In the Middle of the Middle Ages: Integrating Content Standards and the Arts.* By Mary Wheeler and Jill Terlep. Music by Mary Wheeler. Illustrations by Jill Terlep. Westport, CT: Libraries Unlimited/Teacher Ideas Press. Copyright © 2007.

Research Report

Topic Selected: _____

Title of Report: _____

_____

Three Sources of Information:

1. _____

_____

_____

2. _____

_____

_____

3. _____

_____

(List additional sources on another piece of paper.)
Your notes:

_____

_____

_____

_____

_____

(Complete this section once your report is finished.)
Your report contained factual information. Now that it is done, explain how you were affected by what you learned. This section is based on your own ideas, conclusions, beliefs, and feelings.

_____

_____

_____

_____

_____

NAME _____ DATE _____

Tall Cathedrals Touch the Sky

The Middle Ages left an impact on many areas of life, but few are as awe-inspiring as the cathedrals built during that era. Many great cathedrals were constructed from 550 to 1450, and they were immense and complex even by today's standards. By the 1200s, the style that we now call Gothic became common, and those architectural designs are still widely used today.

Below is a list of parts, structural features, and architectural elements of the cathedrals. Some of these components originated with Roman temples or other earlier structures, but all are associated with the cathedrals of the medieval period.

apse—an often semicircular area, usually behind the altar with a half-domed ceiling

flying buttress—an arched support, made of stone, designed to support the heavy walls from the outside of the building

vault—a high, arched masonry structure forming a ceiling, usually covered with a decorative finish; various styles, such as the rib vault, appeared in the Middle Ages

rose window—circular stained-glass window with mullions (slender vertical bars) radiating from the center, attaining greater size and prominence during medieval times

spire—a pointed structure on the top of a building, particularly popular during the Middle Ages, helping cathedrals "touch the sky"

gargoyles—water spouts placed around edges of roof usually carved to appear as a scary figures

nave—a large central area of the cathedral, where the nonclergy gathered

transept—the area of a cathedral perpendicular to the main body of the building, which makes the ground plan cross-shaped or cruciform

triforium—a gallery over the side aisles, usually with no windows; possibly used for maintenance or watching for fire in medieval cathedrals

From *In the Middle of the Middle Ages: Integrating Content Standards and the Arts.* By Mary Wheeler and Jill Terlep. Music by Mary Wheeler. Illustrations by Jill Terlep. Westport, CT: Libraries Unlimited/Teacher Ideas Press. Copyright © 2007.

Using the Internet, books, or periodicals, find a picture(s) that depicts four of these elements. Copy or print the picture and label the features. Or take a photograph of a cathedral or building in your area that showcases the Gothic style and label it.

Extra credit. What is your impression of the architectural style of this building?

_____
_____
_____
_____

NAME _____ DATE _____

Black Death! Comparison Table, Part I

Comparison Table Middle Ages Black Death and 2005 Populations		
Country	**Population 2005**	**Population Rounded to the Nearest Million**
France	60,656,178	
Germany	82,431,390	
Italy	58,103,033	
Portugal	10,566,212	
Spain	40,341,462	
United Kingdom	60,441,457	
United States	295,734,134	

No exact records of death rates were kept during the bubonic plague. The number of people who died in Europe is estimated at one-fourth to one-third of the population. Roughly **20 million** lives were lost to the Black Death in the 14th century.

<u>Compared with the 2005 populations, the lives lost during the plague were</u>

1. almost twice as many as the entire population of _____.

2. nearly one-third the population of _____ and _____.

3. around 38 million less than _____.

4. about one-fifteenth of the _____ population.

5. around 50 percent of the people in _____ .

From *In the Middle of the Middle Ages: Integrating Content Standards and the Arts.* By Mary Wheeler and Jill Terlep. Music by Mary Wheeler. Illustrations by Jill Terlep. Westport, CT: Libraries Unlimited/Teacher Ideas Press. Copyright © 2007.

NAME _____ DATE_____

Black Death! Comparison Table, Part II

Make a bar graph of the loss of lives in the 14th century to Black Death and the populations of the countries listed in the Comparison Table, Part I. Be sure to label each axis, horizontal and vertical.

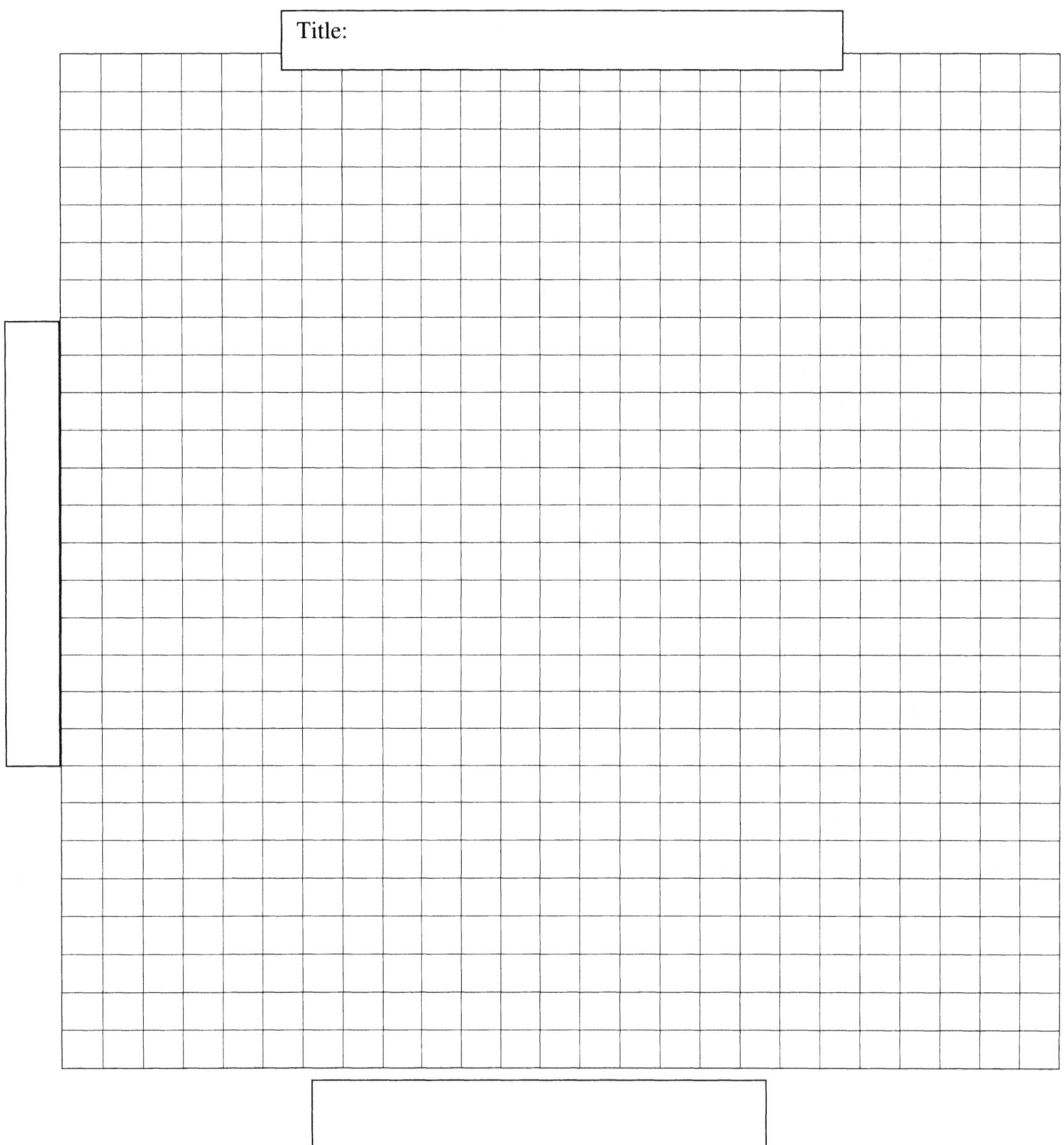

NAME _____ DATE_____

A Dragon, Can You Imagine?

    In medieval folklore, dragons often lived in caves, mountains, or lakes. Stories were told of how they had magical abilities, such as being able to become invisible or change shape. With scaly skin and pointy teeth, the fire-breathing, four-footed creatures spread evil among their mythical victims. Especially during the Middle Ages, the tales of brave knights slaying the winged dragons abounded. Can you imagine it? Draw your version, and write a caption beneath the picture.

From In the Middle of the Middle Ages: Integrating Content Standards and the Arts. By Mary Wheeler and Jill Terlep. Music by Mary Wheeler. Illustrations by Jill Terlep. Westport, CT: Libraries Unlimited/Teacher Ideas Press. Copyright © 2007.

NAME _____ DATE_____

The Normans Are Coming! Details at Eleven

"The Normans are invading England! Details at eleven." Imagine if the Middle Ages were covered by our evening news. Just like today, there would be plenty of exciting information to report.

You could…

Conduct interviews with local serfs using your on-the-scene news crew. Forecast weather for the upcoming village fair, or report "live" from the jousting tournament during the sports. Give a "restaurant" feast review, or prepare a tasty dish for the camera in the lord's kitchen. Broadcast entertainment news on the traveling minstrel's tour, or discuss politics with the king. Need a little gossip news? Share the details of the betrothal announcement of a lord's daughter.

Choose one of the topics listed above or think of your own. Write some questions, and make plans with your team. Do you have an anchor? Oh, yes! Just for fun, your action news will be videotaped.

Write your notes here.

_____
_____
_____
_____
_____
_____
_____
_____
_____
_____
_____
_____
_____
_____
_____
_____

NAME _____ DATE _____

Read All about It

It's a fiction book report about the Middle Ages. Complete the information.

Title: _____

Author: _____

Illustrator: _____

Setting: _____

Place: _____

Time: _____

Three main characters:

    1. _____

    2. _____

    3. _____

Plot: (problem the main character faces)

_____

_____

_____

_____

Three specific events in this book:

    1. _____

_____

_____

    2. _____

_____

_____

    3. _____

_____

Summary

Beginning:

_____
_____
_____
_____
_____
_____
_____
_____

Middle:

_____
_____
_____
_____
_____
_____
_____
_____
_____
_____

End:

_____
_____
_____
_____
_____
_____
_____
_____

Select one or two paragraphs to read aloud to encourage others to read this book, but don't give away the ending! Page ____

NAME _____ DATE _____

Tournament Adventure

Here's the middle of a story about a tournament day in a village in England in the year of 1313. What happened in the beginning and ending? Finish the story.

Title _____

_____
_____
_____
_____
_____
_____
_____
_____
_____

All of a sudden, Sir Edward got off his horse and ran as quickly as he could to the viewing stand!

_____
_____
_____
_____
_____
_____
_____
_____
_____
_____
_____

From *In the Middle of the Middle Ages: Integrating Content Standards and the Arts.* By Mary Wheeler and Jill Terlep. Music by Mary Wheeler. Illustrations by Jill Terlep. Westport, CT: Libraries Unlimited/Teacher Ideas Press. Copyright © 2007.

NAME _____ DATE _____

Heraldry, In the Heat of Battle

    A coat of arms was displayed on the shield to identify a knight when he was wearing a complete suit of armor. With his helmet on his head, no one could tell who he was, and a warrior wouldn't want to attack his friend! Certain rules were followed in the designs. Find the answers to these questions.

On a coat of arms, what …

1. colors were allowed to be used? _____

2. did a crescent symbol indicate? _____

3. did a rose show? _____

4. was the reason the system was named "heraldry"? _____

5. is the dexter? _____

6. is the sinister? _____

7. is the field? _____

8. does it mean when it is "impaled"? _____

9. are other places besides the shield where it is displayed?
   _____

10. Tell some information that you discovered about heraldry.

_____
_____
_____
_____
_____
_____
_____
_____

It's time for you to design your family's coat of arms. Use all of the information that you gathered to create your design. Remember to use only the colors that were allowed in the Middle Ages. (You may want to sketch it on a practice sheet before making your final drawing.)

NAME _____ DATE_____

Come to the Fair, Part I

Following the collapse of the Roman Empire, travel and trade between cities became more difficult. No longer able to rely on a superior system of roads and lacking governmental protection, communities became isolated from one another. However, spurred by the Crusades, commerce slowly began to develop between the East and the West.

In northern Europe and elsewhere, business centers began appearing along the valleys of rivers. Goods, such as furs, honey, fish, spices, cloth, and medicines arrived from busy ports. Perfume, pearls, ivory, leather, silks, and other luxury items were sold, too.

During the Middle Ages, especially in the later years, much of the trading was done at medieval fairs. Merchants brought merchandise from distant places. Booths and stalls were set up in the streets. Villagers sold things they made or grew. Even entertainers, such as acrobats, jugglers, or performing animal acts, were part of the events. Many could not afford to buy but joined in the festivities.

Your Assignment:

You are a merchant planning to set up a booth at a medieval fair. You are picking products to sell. The difference—you can select things from **today's** world or from the **past** to display. Avoid items that need electricity or fuels to power them. Be specific. Don't just say "clothes" or "furniture," for example. Make a list of your goods. *(example: flashlights)*

NAME _____ DATE _____

Come to the Fair, Part II

Read your list to a partner. Listen as your partner reads his or her list to you. Then answer the following questions about <u>your partner's</u> items for sale. (You cannot look at your partner's paper or ask any more questions.)

On your partner's list, what item is the ...

1. biggest?
   _____

2. object that would have received the most attention?
   _____

3. most unusual?
   _____

4. funniest?
   _____

5. best one that you didn't think of?
   _____

6. one that might also have been sold back in the Middle Ages?
   _____

7. most practical item that your partner chose?
   _____

8. thing that would have affected people's lives the most?
   _____

9. most recently invented article?
   _____

10. Who do you think would sell more products, you or your partner? Why?
    _____
    _____
    _____
    _____

NAME _____ DATE _____

Come to the Fair, Part III

Now it's time to organize and display your products. Draw a diagram or an illustration of your booth at the medieval fair. Include activities, stalls, or stores of other festival participants. Where are the streets and businesses located?

NAME _____ DATE_____

Do You Need a Hurdy-Gurdy?

Have you ever heard of a pothook, trivet, or cauldron? A cook in medieval times knew what they were and used them daily. What about a billhook, seedlip, or sickle? Peasants had to have them. Who owned a hurdy-gurdy or a naker? How about a lump hammer? paternoster? trebuchet? All of those objects were tools of the trades.

Select a job from the Middle Ages. Learn about implements or equipment used in that work. Prepare a two-minute presentation to the group. Include at least two audiovisual aids, such as a map, drawing, list, graph, song, or Microsoft PowerPoint presentation.

Topic: _____

Notes:
_____
_____
_____
_____
_____
_____
_____
_____
_____
_____
_____
_____
_____
_____
_____
_____
_____
_____

A Sickle | A Hurdy-Gurdy in Box Form

From In the Middle of the Middle Ages: Integrating Content Standards and the Arts. *By Mary Wheeler and Jill Terlep. Music by Mary Wheeler. Illustrations by Jill Terlep. Westport, CT: Libraries Unlimited/Teacher Ideas Press. Copyright © 2007.*

NAME _____ DATE_____

Picture the Past

In the Middle Ages, illuminations on the pages of the books told stories in elaborately, detailed pictures. Even Johann Gutenberg's Bible was surprisingly beautiful with its colorful drawings. Often, the printed word alone is not enough to give needed information. Graphic sources, such as pictures, drawings, charts, graphs, tables, maps, and diagrams, help the reader understand ideas.

You can describe a halberd on the printed page, but a picture—"It's worth a thousand words." The construction of medieval castles can be explained in detail, but diagrams, drawings, and photographs help us understand them.

What a wonderful array of books we have to choose from! Select a book about the Middle Ages with graphic sources. It may be in the juvenile or adult section of your library. Read it, study it, and enjoy it!

What is the title and author's name?

_____

What is the copyright date?

_____

Color or black/white? _____ Number of pages _____

What size is the book? *(length and width)* _____

What kind of graphic sources does it contain?

_____

_____

_____

How is it arranged? *(pages per topic? types of subjects? graphic sources? etc.)*

_____

_____

_____

_____

_____

_____

_____

_____

From In the Middle of the Middle Ages: Integrating Content Standards and the Arts. By Mary Wheeler and Jill Terlep. Music by Mary Wheeler. Illustrations by Jill Terlep. Westport, CT: Libraries Unlimited/Teacher Ideas Press. Copyright © 2007.

What is a fact that you learned from the book?

_____
_____
_____
_____

What did you like about the pages?

_____
_____
_____
_____
_____
_____

List and define five terms or concepts depicted in the book. *(example: concentric castles, bailiff, etc.)*

_____
_____
_____
_____
_____
_____
_____
_____

What is the title/author of another Middle Ages book with graphic sources that looks interesting?

_____
_____

Why? _____
_____
_____

Extra Credit:
If you were writing your own book, what type of graphic sources would you include?

_____
_____
_____

NAME _____ DATE_____

A Pyramid of Power

In the feudal society a pyramid of power existed with the king at the top and peasants at the base. However, the support was not a clearly defined structure. People might owe allegiance to more than one lord, or their rank could vary within the system.

A Sickle

Because of conditions of the times, feudalism worked in central and western Europe in the Middle Ages. Why would these features of feudal societies prevent the system from succeeding in today's world?

No Strong Central Government

_____
_____
_____
_____
_____
_____

Little Exchange of Money—Trade Goods

_____
_____
_____
_____
_____
_____

Grant Fiefs for Protection

_____
_____
_____
_____
_____
_____

From In the Middle of the Middle Ages: Integrating Content Standards and the Arts. By Mary Wheeler and Jill Terlep. Music by Mary Wheeler. Illustrations by Jill Terlep. Westport, CT: Libraries Unlimited/Teacher Ideas Press. Copyright © 2007.

NAME _____ DATE _____

In the Spirit of the Moment

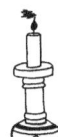 During the Middle Ages, the religions of Buddhism, Christianity, Hinduism, Islam, and Judaism spread to people far beyond the areas where they began. Centuries later, their followers number in the hundreds of millions.

Interview a person of faith.

Plan the interview questions ahead of time. Compose open-ended sentences that require answers beyond a simple "yes" or "no." Begin with words like *"Tell me ...," "Please explain ...,"* or *"Describe ...."* Remember the five Ws—who, what, when, where, and why—when you are writing. The following are examples of topics that you might want to discuss with the person:

- *Describe the basic beliefs of your religion.*
- *Tell me about experiences that have made your faith stronger.*
- *Please explain the important rituals in your religion.*
- *How do others guide you in deepening your faith?*

(If you can tape record your interview and write your report later, you will enjoy the visit more.)

During the interview, be polite to your subject. Respect the person's ideas even if they are different from your own. Not everyone has the same point of view, and much can be learned from one another. After the meeting, write a report about your findings.

Interview

Subject's Name: _____

Subject's Faith: _____

Interview Questions and Answers:

_____
_____
_____
_____
_____
_____
_____
_____
_____
_____

(Continue on a separate piece of paper.)

From In the Middle of the Middle Ages: Integrating Content Standards and the Arts. *By Mary Wheeler and Jill Terlep. Music by Mary Wheeler. Illustrations by Jill Terlep. Westport, CT: Libraries Unlimited/Teacher Ideas Press. Copyright © 2007.*

Gifted and Talented

Consider *In the Middle of the Middle Ages* to be a vehicle transporting student development beyond the traditional classroom. The Teacher Resource section of the book guides the pupils through the history of the Middle Ages, and the Play carries their imaginations and thoughts to new levels. Children truly become excited about the educational trip. Doors open to new avenues for learning. So follow the path of students' interests, and treasure the journeys.

- Are they actors, artists, comedians, teachers, inventors, leaders, debaters, photographers, speakers, musicians, or humanitarians?

- Does the idea of writing, composing, designing, cooking, or sewing excite them?

- What about construction, architecture, woodworking, farming, and education?

- Do they want to learn more about the theatre, ecology, genealogy, or botany?

- Physical activities—are they dancers, competitive athletes, or game players and strategists?

- Are they fascinated by history, philosophy, poetry, geography, religion, science, or mathematics?

When children discover medieval areas of study that excite their curiosity, their learning spirals upward. Encourage them to pursue those interests. For ideas beyond the worksheets, be sure to check the *Cross Curriculum ... More Activities!* section of the book. It's full of great ideas.

During the production of the play, taking advantage of the students' special gifts, inclinations, and talents works out well. If possible, allow some of them to assume responsibilities, either limited or complete, as managers, helpers, and leaders. Think about using children in any of the following jobs:

- Student Director—works with instructor, leads practices, and helps in overall management

- Props Manager—makes sure props are ready, organizes their storage, and ensures that the production runs smoothly

- Music Maestro—conducts the singers and choir in one or more songs, practices with small groups of performers, and provides input for musical performances

- Costume Designer—makes outfits as suggested in the book or fashions patterns and sews better ones

- Choreographer—creates hand motions for choir members and dance steps for songs like *Castle in Motion* and teaches them to participants

Instrumental Musician—plays drums and rhythms and accompanies songs on the piano, fifes, flutes, or other instruments

Set Constructor—builds suggested sets from the book or adds more innovative plans for scenery

Photographer—records activities, practices, and performances for graphic records

Videographer—films practices and performances

Decorator—takes charge of hanging or arranging the displays for the show

Drama Coach—works with small groups or individuals to improve deliveries and memorize lines

Journalist—maintains a written record of the proceedings

Set Artist—creates props and decorations

Sound Manager—runs the amplifiers and sound systems

Lighting Assistant—positions and maintains the spotlights and other lighting effects

The performance of the play is not the end, but the beginning. Celebrate the successes of the children, and challenge them to use their skills and abilities to make a difference. A new page in history is recorded every day.

Cross Curriculum ... More Activities!

Language Arts

Make a newsletter full of fun facts. Enlist the librarian's help in conducting a 30-minute research project with the students. Challenge each pupil to find a fun fact about the Middle Ages that was not learned in class. For example, in the towns, slop pails and chamber pots were emptied out the windows. So watch out when walking down the street! Facts can be divided into categories, such as everyday life, religion, architecture, trade, political life, and so on. Have students write a paragraph on the information that they found. Create a newsletter from all of the newly discovered fun facts. Start the day with this bit of morning news on each desk.

Invite outside speakers to address the class. People to ask might be museum curators, historical society members, tourism officials, local authors, educators, and community experts. Some community members may have firsthand knowledge of castles, cathedrals, or universities that were established in the Middle Ages. They may have lived in or toured the locations. Maybe they even have personal friends or family from the vicinity. Ask them to share and bring any related items, pictures, or presentations. Guests can address the class and then conduct question and answer discussions.

Another possibility is to conduct press conferences with the speakers, if they are comfortable with the arrangement. Set up the classroom like a mini news station. Question the people and record their responses. Follow up the events by writing articles about the invited visitors and topics. Prior to the appearances, discuss respectful behaviors toward visitors.

Employ written communication skills. Compose the following kinds of letters:

invitation—to speakers to address the class or welcome visitors.

thank you—to speakers or anyone who has contributed to the course of study.

query—to individuals or organizations that can provide needed insight or information.

business—when ordering supplies, gathering articles, or other reasons.

friendly—when contacting people on an informal basis, perhaps just telling a relative about the latest Middle Ages facts.

e-mail—if the situation dictates. (These must be strictly monitored.)

Copy the song and poetry lyrics from overhead transparencies. Practice cursive writing, memorize the words, and learn history while writing the poetry. This is a good once- or twice-a-week activity.

Stage a debate. Draw names from a helmet or choose sides to defend whether King John should sign the Magna Carta, William the Conqueror should invade England, a peasant should be allowed to hunt and fish on the lord's property, or Queen Isabella should finance Christopher Columbus's voyage. Research opinions and try to convince others to agree.

Make a list of books and related materials about the Middle Ages that are available in the school or local library. Vote on a passage or book to read together as a group. Post the suggested reading list outside the classroom or in the library for others to enjoy.

Study independently at learning stations. Packets can contain music and rhymes, background information, vocabulary, and worksheets.

Write songs. Become minstrels and entertain the guests in the great hall of the palace.

Write a story about a character in the Middle Ages. It might be about

- a knight preparing for a tournament.
- a woman caring for her family during the Black Death plague.
- a sculptor laboring on the building of a great cathedral.
- a lady tending to the needs of the castle while her husband is away.
- a groom planning for the dowry that he will receive.
- a Crusader telling about what it's like to be away from home.
- a Muslim living in the Holy Land during the Middle Ages.
- a performer at the village fair.

Report on a day in the life of a lady of the manor, a peasant woman, or a merchant's wife.

Design a newspaper advertisement or write a radio or television commercial for a popular product used at the time, such as fine silk from the Mediterranean, wool from England, or resources such as iron, copper, wine, or salt. Show and explain the ad or deliver the commercial to the class.

Compose make-believe journal entries written by fictional or nonfictional characters of the period.

Give a book report in a bag. No, don't get in a bag to deliver it! Select a book about the Middle Ages to read. On a paper sack, write the title and author. Design a book jacket to show what the book is about, and put it in the bag along with 10 items that can be used to report on the book to the class. Pull out one thing at a time as the speech is delivered.

Bring in related artifacts from the era. Have "Show and Tell."

Careers

Rate a job. The lord and lady of the castle needed a staff of full-time workers to maintain the workings of the castle. On a scale of 1 to 10, record personal interest in those jobs that were available: taster, pantler, butler, chief cook, carver, cupbearer, mat weaver, falconer, spinner, groom, sweeper, clerk, steward, priest, marshal, archer, crossbowman, knight, juggler, jester, and musician. Discuss reasons for decisions and numbers. Vote on favorite choices.

Stage a job fair. Provide a list of possible careers that a person held in the Middle Ages. Draw, assign, or have the students select a profession. Research the work. Memorize a two-sentence description of the job and its importance. Set up booths and learn from each participant. Stay "in character" for the event.

Write a medieval resume. Include things such as experience, interests, background, and objectives to apply for that job. Exaggeration is acceptable.

Find out about toys of the period such as hoops, cloth or clay dolls, toy shields, swords, lances, and hobby horses. Start a Middle Ages toy store. Make up a new toy or game appropriate for the time.

Learn more about guilds. With increased trade in the later Middle Ages, guilds were formed to protect the merchants, craftsmen, and consumers. Members set standards for product prices, wages, and quality of products. They set up trade with faraway places as well as locally. Choose a craft: butcher, baker, leather worker, hatter, cobbler, tailor, goldsmith, or other. Explain the job. How does joining the guild help someone be more successful? Write about it.

Art

Build a village typical of medieval times. Choose teams of students to plan the community layouts. Learn about the locations of the crops, peasants' homes, village greens, mills, and castles. Study the topography of early communities. Be resourceful and construct buildings with crayons, markers, pipe cleaners, popsicle sticks, cardboard pieces, and boxes, and use other simple, inexpensive supplies. Display the results.

Design a one-size-fits-all tunic with personal coat-of-arms. *(It will fit any average-sized 12-year-old.)* Cut a rectangular piece of inexpensive material into pieces, two yards by 1 yard. Fold it in half. A slit should be cut in the top, leaving six inches on each side to the shoulder edges. The center part of the slit should be about two inches, front to back. Allow a little extra material so that the neck slot can be hemmed to prevent it from raveling too much. For the coat of arms, cut a rectangle, 15 inches by 12 inches. Draw a shield on it. Sketch a design and use paint or markers to decorate it. When decorating, it's a good idea to mask the rectangle with tape to an aluminum foil covered piece of cardboard. That way, it will remain secure and not bleed through to the work surface. Sew the shield (hem the edges if you wish) to the tunic. Tie the tunic around the waist with a cord.

Make a collage. Include pictures, maps, or other graphic sources in periodicals about the Middle Ages. Add drawings. Display them in a prominent area.

Draw or paint a mural depicting life in medieval times.

Have a "Funnies" contest.

- Make a cartoon about a Middle Ages subject.
- Don't put names on the works.
- Later, number the completed cartoons.
- Scramble the drawings and place them on different student desks.
- "Snake" around the room reading the comic on each desk.
- When the teacher rings a bell or gives a signal, change to the next seat. (Giggle, but don't talk.) It's a quiet activity.
- Note the numbers of three favorite cartoons.
- When everyone has enjoyed all of the drawings, vote on the class's choice as the best.
- Congratulate, give prizes, and display the top three winners' entries.

Make a class booklet. Include the Middle Ages stories and drawings. Share it with another class or visitors to the room. Display it.

Math

Make timelines for the Hundred Years War, the Crusades, lines of royalty, events during the fall of the Roman Empire, changes in Holy Land control, or the spread of the bubonic plague.

Count to 100 in Roman Numerals. Write a relative or adult friend's age and date of birth, the current year, the distance from New York City to Los Angeles, or the jersey number of a favorite NBA, NFL, or NHL player in Roman numerals.

Using a road map, plan an imaginary (or real) car trip to important places of the time: battle sites, cathedrals, castles, universities, or other historical sites.

Calculate the dimensions of a castle of long ago. Figure the circumference of a moat that could have encircled it. Measure a similar area around the school or other structure. How do they compare?

Science, Health, and Nutrition

Prepare a feast. Make it an everyday Middle Ages meal by serving stew in hollowed-out bread bowls, or trenchers. Another option—have a more elaborate feast like a lord of the manor might want when he returned home from a journey. Include roast meat, grilled fish, dried fruit, and cakes with honey. No matter what is served, leave the forks off the table. Eating with fingers is allowed. Have a minstrel entertain during the dining. Plan menus, research recipes, and cook dishes of the era. No peacocks, please! What kinds of herbs were used? How did the people feel about eating onions and garlic? What about serving a meal of flowers, maybe violets and primrose? Have a discussion. Enjoy a Middle Ages dish.

Learn about topics:

- Research medicine and methods of treatment used by medieval people.
- Find out more about the Black Plague.
- Research crops grown on the land, how it was farmed, and common implements used.
- Study medieval habits of sanitation and their effects on quality of lives.
- Learn more about the Great Famine, its causes and effects.
- How did the diets affect the health of the people?
- Compare today's nutritional diets with those of the Middle Ages.

History

Address specific historical questions such as the following:

- What were some of the causes of the rise of Islamic civilization from the seventh century through the late Middle Ages?
- What was Muhammad's life like?
- Why did new ports and merchant communities begin to emerge during this time?
- How did papal power change in its relations between the secular rulers of Europe?
- In what ways were monasteries and convents centers of political power?
- What factors contributed to the weakening of the Roman Empire?
- Where were maritime or overland trade routes located?
- How did ideals of chivalry and courtly love affect feudal society?

Maps

Label and identify the movements or changes of any of these medieval or historical events:

- trade routes, maritime and overland
- Black Death
- Great Famine
- routes of the Crusaders

- Hundred Years War
- Battle of Hastings
- migrations of farming peoples to new European regions
- locations of towns and villages, following the collapse of Roman Empire

Show the boundaries and political regions of the various empires or states: Roman Empire, Medieval Europe at various times, the Mongol Empire, the Byzantine Empire, the Holy Land, and the Crusader states.

Locate architectural or cultural places of interest, such as cathedrals, castles, statues, universities, monasteries, battle sites, and birthplaces of famous figures.

Label physical features of the European lands, such as mountainous regions, river systems, and waterways—lakes, seas, channels, rivers, and ocean.

Discuss geography, physical challenges of the land on trade, and the way the creation of new trade routes affected people's lives.

Answer Key

Middle Ages Overview Questions, page 18

1. Roman Empire
2. Renaissance
3. Roman
4. German
5. Alaric
6. manorial
7. rivers/ streams
8. duke of Normandy/William the Conqueror
9. William the Conqueror
10. Northern France
11. English Channel
12. The Domesday Book
13. Pope Urban II
14. 1096
15. 8
16. 200
17. 7
18. chain mail
19. tournaments
20. once or twice a year
21. feudalism
22. king
23. workers, peasants, and serfs
24. Magna Carta
25. June 15, 1215
26. Henry II
27. Richard the Lion-Hearted
28. 12th and 13th
29. cathedrals
30. Christianity

Traveling Minstrel, page 24

1. jongleurs
2. castles, manors
3. exaggerated
4. great hall
5. knights, barons
6. food, lodging
7. books
8. songs
9. memorized
10. respect

Marching to the Crusades, page 31

1. B	6. C	11. A	16. A
2. C	7. B	12. C	17. C
3. A	8. B	13. C	18. A
4. C	9. C	14. B	19. C
5. A	10. A	15. B	20. B

Pillory on the Village Green, page 41

(any order)
Examples of violations: drunkenness, gambling, swearing, fighting, wife beating, poaching, being a pickpocket, cheating, thievery, being a vagrant, being an unruly servant, breaking castle regulations

1. True
2. False
3. False
4. True
5. False
6. False
7. True
8. True
9. False
10. True
11. True
12. True

This Riddle, page 47

1. 10th century
2. growth of cities and increased trade
3. 1170
4. Pisa, Italy
5. consul in North Africa
6. merchants
7. arithmetic
8. 1202
9. India
10. printing press

next three numbers: 21, 34, 55

Middle Ages Figures, page 64

1. J—(1118–1170)
2. A—(1398–1468)
3. H—(1214–1292)
4. P—(370–410)
5. N—(1340–1400)
6. B—(1181–1226)
7. I—(1138–1227)
8. M—(1167–1216)
9. L—(570–632)
10. C—(1028–1087)
11. F—(1042–1099)
12. G—(1330–1384)
13. E—(1100–1155)
14. K—(1451–1504)
15. O—(1207–1265)
16. D—(849–899)

Bonus: about 58 years

Choose Your Weapons, page 75

Total = $952.05 spent on weapons

Parchment credit # is date of Battle of Hastings,
when duke of Normandy landed his troops in England.

Accept any response for how the lord got his computer.

It's Time, page 77

Event	Date/Approximate Date
Norman Invasion	1066
First Crusade	1096
Geoffrey of Monmouth writes *History of the Kings of Britain*	1100–1155
Reign of Richard the Lionhearted	1157–1199
Magna Carta is signed	1215
Eighth Crusade	1270 or 1271
Fibonacci publishes Liber Abaci	1202
Johann Gutenberg invents printing press	1450s

Johann Gutenburg Was the Best Inventor, page 78

1. opinion
2. fact
3. opinion
4. fact
5. opinion
6. fact
7. opinion
8. fact
9. opinion
10. fact
11. opinion
12. fact
13. opinion

Comparison Table: Middle Ages Black Death and 2005 Populations, page 83

France, 61 million
Germany, 82 million
Italy, 58 million
Portugal, 11 million
Spain, 40 million
United Kingdom, 60 million
United States, 296 million

1. Portugal
2. France, United Kingdom
3. Italy
4. United States
5. Spain

Heraldry, In the Heat of the Battle, page 90

1. red, blue, black, green, purple, silver, gold
2. Second son (family position)
3. Seventh son (family position)
4. People called "heralds" delivered messages to knights on the battlefields
5. right side of shield
6. left side of shield
7. background of the shield
8. two families were combined
9. tunics, flags, banners, seals, gatehouses

Do You Need a Hurdy-Gurdy? page 95

Pothook—used for hanging pots over a fire, curved piece of iron (cook)
Trivet—three-legged stand used for hanging pots over a fire (cook)
Cauldron—large pot used for boiling (cook)
Billhook—tool with curved blade used for cleaning brush (peasant farmer)
Seedlip—pouch that carries seed to be scattered (peasant farmer)
Sickle—tool used for cutting tall grass or grain (peasant farmer)
Hurdy-gurdy—stringed instrument (musician)
Naker—kind of kettledrum (musician)
Lump hammer—heavy hammer used with chisel with cutting stone (stonemason)
Paternoster—large bead on rosary (monk)
Trebuchet—weapon used to hurl large stones through castle walls (soldier)

Answer Key—Crossword Puzzles

Castle Terms Crossword Puzzle, page 54

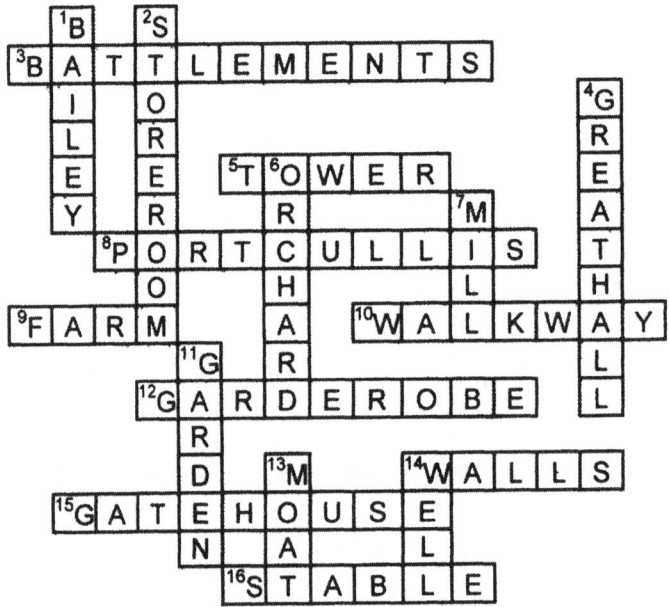

Medieval Terms Crossword Puzzle, page 58

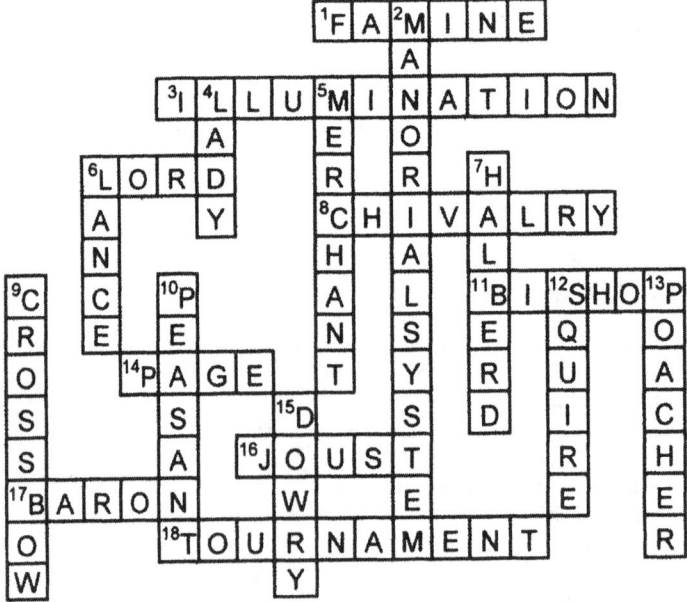

Medieval Figures Crossword Puzzle, page 62

Across:
5. ALFRED THE GREAT
6. MERLIN
8. HENRY
9. THOMAS BECKET
10. DUKE OF NORMANDY

Down:
1. GEOFFREY CHAUCER
2. ROGER BACON
3. KING ARTHUR
4. JOHANN GUTENBERG
7. ALARI

The Play

Play Synopsis

Hungry Herald is a dragon who is befriended by the castle children. They must solve a riddle to help feed poor Herald, who loves bread but never has enough. Traveling through the countryside, Herald and the children learn about life in the middle of the Middle Ages from interesting characters such as the minstrel, a Crusader and his horse, a peasant, and members of King Arthur's Court. Leonardo Pisano, an Italian mathematician who introduces everyone to Arabic numerals and counting, provides the riddle's solution.

Scenes and Musical Sequence

INTRODUCTION
Illuminations (Choir)

ACT 1
Scene 1: Hungry Herald and the Children
Salted Meats and Pickled Beets (Hungry Herald)
Scene 2:
Traveling Minstrel (chorus and first verse, Minstrel)
Illuminations (Choir)

ACT 2
Scene 1: Peasant, Wife, Sir Richard, and Pillory Man
Sun Up, Sun Down (Peasant, his wife, and Stage Characters)
Sir Richard (Sir Richard, Choir, and Stage Characters)
Pillory on the Village Green (Pillory Man)
Scene 2
Traveling Minstrel (chorus and second verse, Minstrel)
Illuminations (Choir)

ACT 3
Scene 1: Crusader, Horse, and King Arthur's Court
Marching to the Crusades (Stage Characters, Horse, and Knight)
Castle in Motion (Guinevere, King Arthur, and Merlin)
Scene 2:
Traveling Minstrel (chorus and third verse, Minstrel)
Illuminations (Choir)

ACT 4 Bride and Leonardo
This Riddle (Stage Characters)
Two Cows (Bride)

FINALE
Magic or Me? (Stage Characters from All Scenes and Choir)

Song Notes

Solos and Special Directions

Switch singers' solos to suit the group. Characters other than those noted can sing many of the songs. When "Stage Characters" are indicated, select a soloist, duet, or any combination of the performers.

Add choreography—dance steps or hand movements—to the songs, especially those done by the choir. They make the musical more enjoyable to perform and watch. Spotlight the choir as they sing.

Illuminations

Choir sings after Scene 2 in Acts 1, 2, and 3.

Salted Meats and Pickled Beets

Herald sings.

Traveling Minstrel

Minstrel sings chorus and one verse each time. Always on stage right, the Minstrel sings the chorus and consecutive verses at the beginning of Scene 2 in Acts 1, 2, and 3.

Illuminations

Choir sings.

Sun Up, Sun Down

Peasant sings verses, and his wife and Stage Characters sing choruses.

Sir Richard

Stage Characters and Choir sing verses. Richard sings chorus.

Pillory on the Village Green

Pillory Man sings.

Traveling Minstrel

Minstrel sings chorus and second verse.

Illuminations

Choir sings.

Marching to the Crusades

Stage Characters sing verses. Horse and Knight sing about the march to the Crusades. Add a "clippity-clop" sound effect by drumming on a wood block or tapping plastic or paper cups on a table.

Castle in Motion

Drummer or keyboard plays 2/4 percussion beat throughout the song. Guinevere or everyone can sing the first verse. King Arthur sings his lines. Guinevere or everyone can introduce Merlin's motions. Merlin can either speak or sing his directions to the dancers. Hidden cue cards for Merlin and the dancers are helpful. Any combination of singers can perform the last lines.

Dancers should practice their choreographed motions. Let the words guide the movements. If the song seems to drag on too long, consider eliminating some of the motions.

Traveling Minstrel

Minstrel sings chorus and last verse.

Illuminations

Choir sings.

This Riddle

Stage Characters sing.

Two Cows

Bride sings. If possible, two cows, or any combination of animals provides a comical effect. They can follow the bride.

Magic or Me?

Everyone sings (including the Stage Hands). When the lights are off, children secretly place the cardboard chest (big enough to hide Herald) in the center of the stage. Herald hides behind it until they sing the word, "Surprise." He pops up. All of the lights are turned on at that time. A black light is not required, but it lends excitement.

White gloves are optional, but they are really effective. Choreograph the motions so the gloves are in front of the children and move a lot. Practice with the black light, and experiment with movements to see what works. Kids love them.

Costumes and Cast of Characters

Factors such as budget, time schedule, performance location, and creative talents determine the kinds of costumes that students wear for the production. Outfits can be as simple or elaborate as your situation dictates.

Buy or Rent

Knights, peasants, lords, and ladies—you can buy or rent all kinds of outfits from a large number of places. If you are in a hurry and have the money, most costume stores in midsize and large cities offer medieval attire for rent and sale. You can also order them via the Internet.

For accessories such as shields or helmets, try the discount stores or children's toy stores. Many sell plastic armor vests for knights and other medieval items.

Sew

Sewing costumes for the production is a great choice, too. Stitch them yourself, or, better yet, enlist the help of parents or friends. Volunteers develop a vested interest in the production, and their talents ensure the program's success. Find patterns for costumes at fabric stores or discount stores. Using the Internet, enter "sewing patterns" into a search engine (e.g., Google) and you will get a huge number of responses. All the major sewing pattern companies and smaller ones, too, are available online. Material can be found in closeout lots online or at local stores. Cheaper yet, ask for donations of materials and patterns. Maybe someone already has just what you need.

Design Your Own

If you or another creative person wants to design the costumes, try it. Let imaginations and talents guide the way. They don't have to be of Broadway quality, but if they are, take special pride.

Gloves and Black Light

Gloves for the finale are optional. If you decide to use them, you can order them on the Internet. Buy a dozen pairs or more, and the price is very reasonable. They can also be purchased at uniform apparel stores. Military personnel, parade marchers, hospital workers, and coin collectors often use the gloves.

Black theatrical lights are available in a wide range of sizes and prices. (Permanent fixtures can be expensive!) You can buy or rent them at costume stores. Another idea—borrow one from a local theater group. Many are just gathering dust in storage closets.

Simple and Easy-to-Make Costumes

Narrator (Girl or Boy): Optional dress—Wear regular dress-up clothes or same costume as palace children or knight.

Hungry Herald, the Dragon: Wear oversized, dark, hooded sweatshirt and sweatpants. Glue ladder scales on the center of the back. On the hood, glue cardboard eyes and horns. Don't cover the face. Add a tail made of felt or cardboard or any suitable material.

Palace Children (four, can be more or less): Girls—Wear plain-colored, long skirt and peasant blouse; white cloth (dishtowel) over the hair. Boys—Wear dark sweatpants and sweatshirt with a cord tied around the waist.

Minstrel: Same as palace children

Peasant: Same as palace children

Peasant's Wife: Same as palace children

Sir Richard, a knight: Tunic—Measure a rectangle large enough to cover shoulder to legs, and double it. Cut an oval slit for the neck. Tie a cord around the waist. *(See Cross Curriculum, "Art," for additional instructions.)* Glue or sew triangles at the hem of the cloth. Or, for a vest, cover a piece of cardboard with aluminum foil, and draw scales like chain mail on it. Cover a plastic helmet with aluminum foil or paint it silver. Make a shield from heavy cardboard.

Pillory Man: Same as palace children. Make a pillory from cardboard, two vertical beams and horizontal beam with holes for head and hands. Paint to make it board-like.

Crusader: Wear a black tunic with a white cross, signifying Knights Hospitaller. Can carry a matching shield.

Horse: Wear over-sized, brown, hooded sweatshirt and regular sweatpants. Glue felt or cardboard ears and eyes on the hood. Add fringe on the back of the hood for a mane and a horsetail. Add white socks on hands and feet for hooves.

King Arthur: Same as knight, but wear a cardboard crown.

Guinevere: Wear a long skirt or dress, can be fancy; cover hair with material and have a long veil.

Merlin, the Magician: Wear a cardboard pointed hat with stars and moons on it and a big satiny shirt.

Dancers, *Castle in Motion*: Same as palace children

Bride: Same as palace children, or dress as a bride with a net veil.

Leonardo: Same as palace children

Any Actors: Wear a cloak or even a blanket to hide clothes or for costume effect.

Choir: If using the black light, choir members wear white shirts to add to the glove effect. But, if you only want the hands to show, make sure no one in the choir wears white. Another idea—dress like palace children because of song choreography. Or wear tunics like the knights. *(See Cross Curriculum, "Art," on specific directions to make them.)* Finally, wear white shirts or dress up clothes.

Stage Hands: Dark clothing, or black T-shirts with printed words on the front, "Stage Hand."

Props

Illumination poster (optional)
Sound effects for Herald's stomach rumbling and clippity-clop in *Marching to the Crusades*
Drummer or percussion keyboard for *Castle in Motion*
Bread
Scroll with Narrator's copy of Illuminations poem (all verses) on it
Scrolls with "The End" and "Cheer" for the finale
Number cards and scroll for Leo
Spade or tools for Peasants
Pillory (made from heavy brown cardboard)
Shields for Sir Richard and Crusaders
Two cows and animals for Bride (optional)
Treasure chest for Herald to hide behind or inside
White gloves for cast and choir
Blacklight

Backdrop

The play can be performed without any backdrop. However, scenery makes the show more interesting. Because the children are traveling about the countryside, a palace in the background or a general country scene is appropriate. It can be teacher or student made. Paint large pieces of strong cardboard or even a blue bed sheet. If you use the sheet, attach it to a frame to keep it from fluttering.

Stage Setup

The stage is divided into two or three sections:
- Stage right—(optional) Introduction and Scene 2 in Acts 1–3
- Center stage—Scene 1 in Acts 1–4
- Stage left—Scene 2 in Acts 1–3

(Choice: If space and timing allow, the Narrator can speak on stage right and the Minstrel on stage left. Or both can be on the same side and Minstrel follows Narrator.)

Stage Diagram

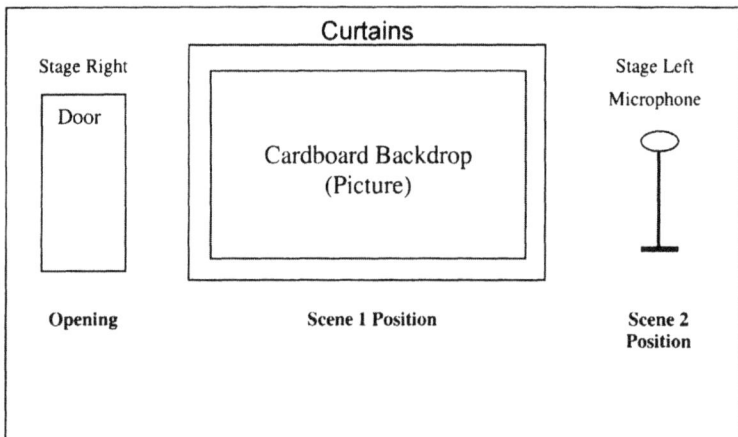

From In the Middle of the Middle Ages: Integrating Content Standards and the Arts. *By Mary Wheeler and Jill Terlep. Music by Mary Wheeler. Illustrations by Jill Terlep. Westport, CT: Libraries Unlimited/Teacher Ideas Press. Copyright © 2007.*

Play Performance Tips

Double Cast

Consider having two sets of the main characters: Hungry Herald and the Palace Children. Even the Minstrel and Narrator can be switched. This plan works well and gives more students an opportunity. Assign one group to Acts 1 and 2, and the second set to Acts 3 and 4.

All the characters appear in the Finale.

Copies of the Script

Adult volunteers can save a lot of time for you at the copy machine and are glad to help.

If your class is **reading the play aloud** and not performing for an audience, you will need enough copies of the entire play for each one or two students. Collect the stapled scripts at the end of the drama, and store them for next year.

For an **audience performance,** complete or partial scripts can be handed out.

- Main characters—Herald, Palace Children, Narrator, and Minstrel—need all the pages. If you have two sets of main characters, give Introduction, Acts 1, 2, and Finale to the first group and Acts 3, 4, and Finale to the second.
- Secondary characters—Peasant, Wife, Sir Richard, Pillory Man, and so on—require only the sheets with their dialogues.
- Every performer—stage characters and choir—should have copies of all of the song words.

All of the students will learn about the Middle Ages through watching and performing.

If you intend to produce the play again next year, you may want to consider collecting all of the scripts at the end. Warn the children ahead of time if you expect them to return their copies when the play is over. (And plan on a few being lost or missing a few pages!)

Add or Eliminate Speakers and Songs

If additional students need to be involved, include more Palace Children, Peasants, Wives, Crusaders, Knights with Sir Richard, and Animals for the bride's dowry. Conversational lines can be added to the script to create more speaking parts. Announcers can welcome the audience and introduce the program, cast, and crew. Eliminate act(s) if not enough students are available. Actors can perform dual roles. Songs can be eliminated, too.

Presentation

Include dance steps or arm movements to go along with the choir music. Choreography makes the songs more enjoyable for the singers and more fun to watch.

When actors are not performing, they join the choir instead of remaining backstage. "Secret" traveling is done when the spotlight is on the opposite side of the stage. Children are responsible for their own moving times.

Stage a dress rehearsal for the whole school. Other classes can learn about the Middle Ages, too!

Practice at least once with the spotlight(s) and microphones. Do a sound check and make sure all of the wires are plugged in.

Flexible Songs

Soloists are suggested, but change the singers to fit the individual class. Transpose the music for more suitable key ranges.

Make cue cards for the song *Castle in Motion* to give the dancers early notice of each new motion or verse. Cue cards should be unseen by the audience and have words like *row a boat, swim a moat, round the table, ride a horse,* and so on.

Student Instrumental Soloist(s) and Performers

The *Traveling Minstrel* song, performed between Acts, is a terrific place to showcase budding talents. A student plays the accompaniment on a guitar, flute, or other instrument; dance; juggles like a jester; or performes another entertaining talent.

Actors' Deliveries and Traveling

Caution students about "upstaging." When another cast member is speaking or singing, all others onstage should remain still. Encourage the actors to speak slowly and clearly and make eye contact often with the audience.

At the end of each Act, the main characters should exit stage right. Spotlight goes off as they move, and turns on to the Narrator and Minstrel. When Scene 2s are finished, the spotlight remains off as all main characters take their places at center stage.

Videotape

Make sure the camera person sees a rehearsal to understand where the action will take place on stage. Let the parents know ahead of time that they don't have to tape the entire program themselves. Each parent should sign a permission slip allowing his or her child to be taped at the performance.

Stage Background (if you want more than is required for the play)

If your stage is bare and uninteresting, you may want to dress it up a bit. Hanging in large letters, *In the Middle of the Middle Ages,* can add balance and interest and brighten it up. Streamers, available at most party stores, or other distinctive, decorative banners can be used for added cover. Large illumination posters can be placed in the background.

Helpers

Enlist as many as possible—other teachers (especially art and music), upper-grade students, parents, secretaries, administrators, language arts and social studies teachers, community members, and so on. It is amazing how much help is available once the word is out. Parents do a terrific job of running spotlights, taking videotape orders, helping build backdrops, managing sound systems, and making costumes. High school students make wonderful choreographers.

Posters

Let the group decorate advertisements for the program. They can be made on poster board or construction paper. Distribute them throughout the school and community.

Programs

Include the children's names on the programs. They make great souvenirs. Students can submit drawings or computer-generated pictures for the program covers.

Publicity

Check with administrators to see whether it's OK to alert local news sources about the presentation. Invite reporters to take pictures and write about the upcoming program. It's positive news about the school.

Timelines

Have the students make timelines about speeches, battles, or events that occurred during the Middle Ages. Plan a collective class timeline, one event per person. Display them during practices and on performance day for the audience.

Invitations

Write letters to the school board, parents, administrators, school staff, and other classes inviting them to attend. Practice good letter writing techniques.

Reception and Wrap Party

A reception is a great way to celebrate post-production enthusiasm. Following the performance, invite family members to join the cast and crew for coffee, punch, and snacks. A parents' group might be interested in organizing and hosting this event.

It's a wrap! During the next available day at school, rejoice together with a party. Watch the video, eat popcorn or treats, discuss the program, give pats on the backs, and have fun!

Off, Off, Off Broadway Singers

Encourage the group to have fun with the music. It's great if the students are always on pitch, but it rarely happens with the normal school group. So tell them to sing out and sing as best they can. The results are often off-key, but the experience is positively unforgettable (and will definitely make you smile!). With families and friends, you have a great biased audience that won't notice the "klinkers."

Homeschool Suggestions for the Play

Include the arts in the children's educational curriculum. Using this unique approach to teaching the history of the Middle Ages stimulates students' academic and developmental growth. Because the play *In the Middle of the Middle Ages* uses simple props and backdrops, it can easily be adapted to most homeschool programs.

Adjust the material for small groups. Stage just one or two acts. Read the play aloud, and include any willing family members or neighbors as participants. Even the family pet can be written into the script. (How about the castle dog?)

Work with other families. Split the responsibilities for backdrops and props among other homeschool groups. Give Act 1 to one family, Act 2 to another, or divide the play to suit the group's size.

Separate children by age. What fits the situation? Have older students perform the main characters' roles. Dancers in *Castle in Motion* can be young children.

In Act 2, along with Sir Richard, let smaller ones, dressed as knights, accompany him. Sir Richard or others sing the first verse, but even preschool students can memorize the lines, starting with "When Richard was a little boy …"

Very young students, dressed as knights, can sing the *Sir Richard* song. A few sentences about the Middle Ages, spoken by different children, can be an entire program. Include the *Castle in Motion* tune, sung by older pupils and performed by younger ones, and you have yet another adaptation.

Invite neighbors, church members, family, and friends to view the finished production. It's a great way for the children to share their talents and knowledge.

Create an auditorium. With simple backdrops, the play can be performed in a backyard, using the side of a house or a deck as the backstage. Sweep out the garage and use sheets to cover the lawn tools. Seat the audience in lawn chairs or on old blankets on the floor like a picnic. Ask the church, civic center, or public library for use of their meeting room. Many will let groups use the space for free. Use a home living room or den. Changing the area into a theater will be part of the fun.

Look for field trip opportunities. Search out museums, collections, and cultural attractions in the local area that feature Middle Ages figures, lifestyles, and experiences. Extend the learning adventure by planning the destination of the next vacation to include architecture that exemplifies the styles seen in the Middle Ages.

Let the book be a springboard that allows the children's natural learning curiosity to leap in new directions.

In the Middle of the Middle Ages

INTRODUCTION

(Spotlight on stage right.)

Narrator: The pages of the books in the Middle Ages were decorated with colorful designs or pictures called illuminations. The illuminations were drawn by hand, and they lit up or called attention to sections. In our play we illuminate the Middle Ages history of long ago.

Narrator: *(reads)*

Illuminations

A law and order government—they organized it well.

Their principles lived on although the Roman Empire fell.

Years of devastating wars

Passed as towns grew on the shores

In the middle of the Middle Ages.

A conqueror named William, ten sixty-six was crowned.

His ruthlessness and courage throughout Europe were renowned.

Into England, Norman's came;

Lots of land the Duke would claim

In the middle of the Middle Ages.

(Sing *Illuminations*)

Illuminations

Illuminations are decorations on the pages of the books of yesterday.

Illuminations—Learn information.

Let us see how others used to work and play.

From *In the Middle of the Middle Ages: Integrating Content Standards and the Arts.* By Mary Wheeler and Jill Terlep. Music by Mary Wheeler. Illustrations by Jill Terlep. Westport, CT: Libraries Unlimited/Teacher Ideas Press. Copyright © 2007.

Illuminations

Mary Wheeler

1. A law and order government-they organized it well.
Their principles lived on although the Roman Empire fell.
Years of devastating wars
Passed as towns grew on the shores
In the middle of the Middle Ages.

2. A Conqueror named William, 1066 was crowned.
His ruthlessnesss and courage throughout Europe were renowned.
Into England, Normans came;
Lots of land the Duke would claim
In the middle of the Middle Ages.

3. 1095's when Christians began the First Crusade.
A journey to Jerusalem to win it back was made.
Eight Crusades, two hundred years -
Even children volunteered
In the middle of the Middle Ages.

4. His loyalty and service was promised to a lord.
The knight, a mighty warrior, could fight with lance and sword.
First, a page and then a squire,
Chain mail was his safe attire
In the middle of the Middle Ages.

5. The tournaments provided a show where knights were trained.
Magnificent occasions - noble families entertained.
Everyone liked village fairs.
Merchants came and sold their wares
In the middle of the Middle Ages.

6. A pyramid of power - the king was at the top.
Below him came the vassals, knights, and serfs who farmed the crops.
As the strong protected weak,
Feudalism reached its peak
In the middle of the Middle Ages.

7. King John had opposition; he went to Runnymeade.
He signed the Magna Carta, but reluctantly agreed.
1215 was when they met.
Liberties were what they'd get
In the middle of the Middle Ages.

8. A Lionhearted Richard and Henrys one, two, three
Were all among the heirs who served as English royalty.
With education on the rise
Tall cathedrals touched the sky
In the middle of the Middle Ages.

From *In the Middle of the Middle Ages: Integrating Content Standards and the Arts.* By Mary Wheeler and Jill Terlep. Music by Mary Wheeler. Illustrations by Jill Terlep. Westport, CT: Libraries Unlimited/Teacher Ideas Press. Copyright © 2007.

*(Spotlight **on stage right**.)*

Narrator: The Middle Ages began with the fall of the Roman Empire in the 5th century and continued to the 1500s. During that time, many castles were built as fortresses. What if a dragon lived in a castle? Watch our play, *In the Middle of the Middle Ages,* to find out what might have happened.

(Spotlight off. Narrator exits stage right.)

Act 1: Hungry Herald and the Children

Scene 1

*(Spotlight **on center stage**. All characters walk to front. If using a background, characters should come from behind it.)*

Child 1: This bread tastes good. I'm happy that we were able to find it.

Child 2: Sometimes, even if I eat my trencher—you know, the bread bowl—I am still hungry a little while after the last meal of the day is finished.

Child 3: The mid-morning and evening meal served by our cooks do not always satisfy me either. Even though our main meal lasts a long time, I still want something to eat later.

Child 4: I look forward to the day that the lord of the castle returns. We'll have a great feast, with more than just stew and bread to eat. We'll have singing and dancing and....

(rumble noise offstage)

Child 1: Listen! I hear something.

Child 2: I hear it, too!

Child 3: It sounds spooky.

(Rumble gets louder.)

Child 2: I am afraid to watch. *(covers eyes)*

Child 4: I am afraid to hear. *(covers ears)*

(Herald, the dragon appears. First, he shows his foot, and gradually, all of him comes into view. The children grab each other and shake with fear.)

Child 1: It is a **ferocious** dragon, and he is growling and mean.

Child 2: *(looks at Herald)* You are a dragon! *(looks at other children)* But, everybody knows that there is no such thing as a dragon.

Child 3: Of course not, dragons are myths, legendary creatures. Even if it were a dragon, legend says that it would live in an underground lair, not a castle.

Child 4: I don't know. He has wings, and *(squinting)* maybe scales. Does he breathe fire? That's the real test.... Dragons definitely breathe fire. Hmmm.... I don't see fire.... Well, maybe I do. I don't know.

Child 3: Oh, please.... Let's just ask him. Excuse me, why are you growling and grumbling?

Herald: Oh, I am not growling with my mouth. I am growling with my stomach. *(pats stomach)* I did not mean to frighten you, children, but I cannot get my stomach to quit grumbling. You see. I have a problem. I'll tell you about it.

(Sing *Salted Meats and Pickled Beets*)

Salted Meats and Pickled Beets

Hungry Herald! Hungry Herald!
But my favorite when I'm fed, have I said, is bread.

I eat what all the castle eats
Like bacon, cod, and salted meats.
Pheasant, partridge, mutton, hare—
Their spicy odors fill the air.

Hungry Herald! Hungry Herald!
But my favorite when I'm fed, have I said, is bread.

I eat what all the castle eats,
And peacocks are their favorite treats.
Salted butter, eggs, hard cheese—
I often eat a lot of these.

Hungry Herald! Hungry Herald!
But my favorite when I'm fed, have I said, is bread.

I eat what all the castle eats
Like puddings, pears, and pickled beets.
Salmon, honey, apples, stew—
I wash them down with ale I brew.

Hungry Herald! Hungry Herald!
But my favorite when I'm fed, have I said, is bread.

Salted Meats and Pickled Beets

Mary Wheeler

From *In the Middle of the Middle Ages: Integrating Content Standards and the Arts*. By Mary Wheeler and Jill Terlep. Music by Mary Wheeler. Illustrations by Jill Terlep. Westport, CT: Libraries Unlimited/Teacher Ideas Press. Copyright © 2007.

Child 3: We feel sorry for you, Herald, but we do not have any more bread. We ate it all just now.

Herald: I need lots of loaves, lots and lots and lots of loaves! I just don't know how much bread I need. It isn't ever enough.

Child 4: I'm always hungry, too, Herald. Always, always, always… If tonight were the night of a feast, we'd still be eating. Mmm, pheasant, pickled beets, roast salmon with creamy sauce … *(trails off, looking dreamy)*

Herald: *(sings sadly)* Hungry Herald …

Child 2: It's OK, Herald. We'll think of something. We won't let you go to bed hungry.

(Traveling Minstrel enters.)

Child 1: Hey, everyone. It's the traveling minstrel who just arrived at the castle this morning. He's going to entertain in the great hall for the dinner. I love to hear him sing about how brave our knights are.

Child 3: I'm sure he'll sing about chivalry. Our knights aren't just brave. They are honorable, respectful, and protect the weak. They follow a strict code of honor. That's being chivalrous.

Minstrel: Hi, children. I overheard your trouble, and I would like to help you feed poor Hungry Herald. Listen to my riddle, and if you can solve it, then you will feed Herald enough bread. Here it is:

> *Take a trip so you can learn.*
> *Hungry Herald should return*
> *After symbols; it's okay.*
> *Rumble, grumble goes away.*

Child 3: *(scratches head, puzzled)* I don't know what the answer to the riddle is, but let's all try to solve it.

Child 4: I love to find answers to problems. This will be fun.

Child 2: We can figure out the answer to getting you more bread, Herald. We'll help you.

Child 1: Let's all walk to the village, and maybe we'll solve it on the way.

*(Spotlight **off**. Characters exit stage left.)*

Scene 2

*(Spotlight **on stage right**. Minstrel is on stage.)*

(Sing *Traveling Minstrel*, chorus and first verse)

Traveling Minstrel

A traveling minstrel, my job is to sing. From castle to manor I go.
I entertain ladies and lords and their guests. Always, I put on a good show.

While the people are feasting, I am singing my songs.
Later, all of them dance to music I play along.

Traveling Minstrel

Mary Wheeler

From *In the Middle of the Middle Ages: Integrating Content Standards and the Arts.* By Mary Wheeler and Jill Terlep. Music by Mary Wheeler. Illustrations by Jill Terlep. Westport, CT: Libraries Unlimited/Teacher Ideas Press. Copyright © 2007.

(Minstrel exits. Narrator enters.)

Narrator: *(reads)*

Ten ninety-five's when Christians began the First Crusade.

A journey to Jerusalem to win it back was made.

Eight Crusades, two hundred years—

Even children volunteered

In the middle of the Middle Ages.

His loyalty and service were promised to a lord.

The knight, a mighty warrior, could fight with lance and sword.

First, a page and then a squire,

Chain mail was his safe attire

In the middle of the Middle Ages.

*(Sing **Illuminations**)*

Illuminations are decorations on the pages of the books of yesterday.

Illuminations—Learn information.

Let us see how others used to work and play.

Illuminations

Mary Wheeler

Il-lu-min-a-tions are dec-or-a-tions on the pa-ges of the books of yes-ter-day.

Il-lu-min-a-tions - Learn in-for-ma-tion let us learn how oth-ers used to work and play.

1. A law and order government-they organized it well.
Their principles lived on although the Roman Empire fell.
Years of devastating wars
Passed as towns grew on the shores
In the middle of the Middle Ages.

2. A Conqueror named William, 1066 was crowned.
His ruthlessnesss and courage throughout Europe were renowned.
Into England, Normans came;
Lots of land the Duke would claim
In the middle of the Middle Ages.

3. 1095's when Christians began the First Crusade.
A journey to Jerusalem to win it back was made.
Eight Crusades, two hundred years -
Even children volunteered
In the middle of the Middle Ages.

4. His loyalty and service was promised to a lord.
The knight, a mighty warrior, could fight with lance and sword.
First, a page and then a squire,
Chain mail was his safe attire
In the middle of the Middle Ages.

5. The tournaments provided a show where knights were trained.
Magnificent occasions - noble families entertained.
Everyone liked village fairs.
Merchants came and sold their wares
In the middle of the Middle Ages.

6. A pyramid of power - the king was at the top.
Below him came the vassals, knights, and serfs who farmed the crops.
As the strong protected weak,
Feudalism reached its peak
In the middle of the Middle Ages.

7. King John had opposition; he went to Runnymeade.
He signed the Magna Carta, but reluctantly agreed.
1215 was when they met.
Liberties were what they'd get
In the middle of the Middle Ages.

8. A Lionhearted Richard and Henrys one, two, three
Were all among the heirs who served as English royalty.
With education on the rise
Tall cathedrals touched the sky
In the middle of the Middle Ages.

From In the Middle of the Middle Ages: Integrating Content Standards and the Arts. By Mary Wheeler and Jill Terlep. Music by Mary Wheeler. Illustrations by Jill Terlep. Westport, CT: Libraries Unlimited/Teacher Ideas Press. Copyright © 2007.

(Spotlight off. Narrator exits. Children and Herald walk to center.)

Act 2: Peasant, Wife, Sir Richard, and Pillory

Scene 1

(Spotlight on center stage.)

Child 1: I can't wait until we have another village fair. Last time, I got to watch the acrobats. They were amazing when they leaped and did their tricks.

Child 2: I enjoy the dancing and the music.

Child 3: I look forward to seeing all of the people from the village.

(Enter Peasant and Wife.)

Peasant: Hi, children, where are you going today?

Child 4: We are going to the village to help our friend, Herald, find some bread to eat.

Peasant: You are not likely to find any extra bread in the village. Each household bakes its own bread. Even during a good harvest year, like this one, there is not much left over.

Child 3: Who makes your bread for your family? Maybe we could ask them to help us make bread for Herald.

Peasant's Wife: I bake the bread. I also make the cheese and butter, feed some of the livestock, milk the cows, clean the house, make the meals, and, of course, care for our children.

Child 4: You have so many duties. It's amazing that you can get it all done.

Peasant's Wife: That's not all I do. I make rope, spin thread, sew clothing, tend the garden, make candles, and get the water from the well.

Peasant: When the children are old enough, they begin helping with the duties in the household. Our children also work with me in the field, scaring birds from the crops, pulling weeds, and helping with the planting and the harvest.

Peasant's Wife: Oh, I work alongside my husband in the field, too, when I get the chance.

Child 2: Your life sounds very hard.

Peasant's Wife: It is hard, but it is satisfying work. We are proud of all that we accomplish.

Peasant: Hard work can have great rewards.

(Sing Sun Up, Sun Down)

Sun Up, Sun Down

Sun up, sun down—in the shadow of the castle he stays.
Sun up, sun down—he's a peasant in medieval days.

(Peasant)
I work in the field with my sickle and spade
And cart the grain back to the mill.
I pay the lord's taxes then tend to my sheep,
And I suffer the cool, autumn chill.

Sun up, sun down—in the shadow of the castle he stays.
Sun up, sun down—he's a peasant in medieval days.

(Peasant)
My dark, one-room home's built of wattle and daub,
The roof made of reeds, tied and straight.
I look to my lord for protection from harm.
It's my life on the feudal estate.

Sun up, sun down—in the shadow of the castle he stays.
Sun up, sun down—he's a peasant in medieval days.
Sun up, sun down—he's a peasant in medieval days.

Sun Up, Sun Down

Mary Wheeler

From *In the Middle of the Middle Ages: Integrating Content Standards and the Arts*. By Mary Wheeler and Jill Terlep. Music by Mary Wheeler. Illustrations by Jill Terlep. Westport, CT: Libraries Unlimited/Teacher Ideas Press. Copyright © 2007.

Child 1: Thank you for telling us about your lives.

Child 4: And thank you for all that you do to support the castle. We didn't know how hard life could be in the village.

Peasant: Good luck finding bread for your friend.

Peasant's Wife: We don't like to see anyone go hungry.

Child 3: Good day to you.

(Peasant and Wife nod good-bye and exit.)

Child 2: I think of the village as a place of fairs, festivals, and merchants. I didn't realize that the peasants in the village had such a hard life.

Child 1: We should be thankful for the safety and security of the castle walls.

Child 4: Yes, we are lucky.

(Sir Richard enters from one side of the stage. Herald enters from the other.)

Sir Richard: Hello, there. I'm Sir Richard.

Child 2: It is an honor to meet you, Sir Richard. Are you a knight?

Sir Richard: Yes, I am…. Is that a dragon? *(looking skeptical)*

Herald: I am Hungry Herald. I am a dragon, but you don't need to slay me. I am friendly, very friendly, and hungry, too.

Sir Richard: Okay. *(nodding and still looking confused)*

Child 4: How did you become a knight? Were you brave? Are you chivalrous? I'd really, really like to be a knight!

Sir Richard: *(focusing back on the children)* I was dubbed a knight in a ceremony, but some knights are dubbed on the battlefield after showing great bravery. You have to be brave to be a knight and follow the code of honor called chivalry.

Child 3: What is chivalry, Sir Richard?

Sir Richard: Chivalry is the code of honor by which knights live. We protect the weak, show respect to women, and fight for our causes.

Child 4: I saw a wonderful tournament where the knights were jousting. Is jousting a cause?

Sir Richard: Jousting is part of a tournament, not a cause. A knight's main jobs are to fight in battles or wars and participate in tournaments. The joust is a way to show people your skills on horseback and with a lance.

Child 1: *(pointing at Sir Richard's shield)* Is that the shield you use in battle? What do the cross and the waves mean? Why do you have a star in the center?

Sir Richard: *(pointing to each part as he identifies it)* The cross is from my father's coat-of-arms and the waves are from my mother's coat-of-arms. I am the second son, which is why I have a star in the center. My older brother inherited the coat-of-arms without any changes. This organized system of badges and symbols is called heraldry. With a coat-of-arms on the shield, knights can tell who their friends are in a battle … and who their enemies are, too!

Hungry Herald: *(very excitedly)* My name is *Herald* because my mother and father are painted on the shield of Lord Robert. They were so excited about being a part of the heraldry that they named *me* Herald!

Child 2: Sir Richard, we know the steps that you had to take to become a knight. *(All children nod heads.)*

Child 3: This is what you did.

(Sing *Sir Richard*)

Sir Richard

He promised to be faithful and protect him with a sword,
And before the altar, vowed to serve the manor of his lord.
He studied hard, and finally, in a solemn feudal rite –
A nobleman, a vassal—he was dubbed a trusted knight.

When Richard was a little boy, he was called a page.
He became a squire next at fourteen years of age.
At last, he turned into a knight, and he was very proud.
He loved to say his name and said it many times aloud.

Sir Richard, Sir Richard, Sir Richard is my name.
Sir Richard, Sir Richard, Sir Richard is my name.
Sir Richard, Sir Richard, Sir Richard is my name.
Sir Richard, Sir Richard, Sir Richard is my name.

Sir Richard

Mary Wheeler

Child 4: I can see why you wanted to say your name over and over again. I hope that I can be a knight someday, too. I'll say my name, too.

Child 1: Thank you for explaining heraldry and chivalry to us. We can see why you were dubbed a knight, Sir.

Sir Richard: You're welcome. Continue to follow a code of honor and you'll make your manor proud.

(Sir Richard exits. Pillory and Man are secretly moved into stage left.)

Child 4: Oh, I want to be a knight. I really, really want to be a knight.

*(Spotlight **on stage left**. Children walk over to talk to Pillory Man.)*

Child 2: That man is locked in the pillory. I know I'd never commit a crime. I wouldn't want to be punished like that.

Pillory Man: This is bad. I agree, but it could have been worse. Others are imprisoned in the dungeon. I have to spend one day in the pillory for cheating. The local lord felt this sentence fit my crime. I have learned my lesson.

Child 3: We know that it is wrong to cheat. I'm glad you know now, too.

Herald: It would be hard to find a pillory to fit a dragon.

Pillory Man: I didn't even think dragons existed. I must really deserve punishment for my crimes for the local lord to send a dragon to me, too.

(Sing Pillory on the Village Green)

Pillory on the Village Green

It was a crime I didn't mean,
And now each passerby has seen
My head and hands and legs between
These timbers on the village green.

I hid my face as I was led
To village green and sadly said,
"I nevermore will get ahead
By cheating; I'll be fair instead."

Ha! Ha! Ha! Hee! Hee! Hee! I know it isn't funny, but you see—
Ha! Ha! Ha! Hee! Hee! Hee! I'm laughing 'cause it tickles on my knee.

When my nose was twitching
I could use my hands for itching,
But my hands can't reach to scratch my knee.

Ha! Ha! Ha! Hee! Hee! Hee! I know it isn't funny, but you see—
Ha! Ha! Ha! Hee! Hee! Hee! I'm laughing 'cause it tickles on my knee.

Would you scratch that little tickle on my knee?

Pillory on the Village Green

Mary Wheeler

From *In the Middle of the Middle Ages: Integrating Content Standards and the Arts*. By Mary Wheeler and Jill Terlep. Music by Mary Wheeler. Illustrations by Jill Terlep. Westport, CT: Libraries Unlimited/Teacher Ideas Press. Copyright © 2007.

From *In the Middle of the Middle Ages: Integrating Content Standards and the Arts.* By Mary Wheeler and Jill Terlep. Music by Mary Wheeler. Illustrations by Jill Terlep. Westport, CT: Libraries Unlimited/Teacher Ideas Press. Copyright © 2007.

Herald: Here, I'll scratch your knee for you. I like to scratch. I scratch all the time. See? *(Henry scratches himself all over, even his backside. Then he scratches the knee of the Pillory Man.)*

Pillory Man: Thanks a lot! It's much better now. I'm embarrassed at being in here. I was drawn to the pillory for baking short-weight loaves of bread. My fines will be heavy, but I am lucky to have learned my lesson.

Child 2: Yes, sir. We've all learned a lesson. We won't cheat anyone either.

Child 4: Or do anything else… That dungeon sounds scary, not the place for me. *(trails off as they exit)*

(Spotlight *off*. *Characters exit.*)

Scene 2

*(Spotlight **on stage right.** Minstrel is on stage.)*

(Sing ***Traveling Minstrel,*** chorus and second verse)

Traveling Minstrel

A traveling minstrel, my job is to sing. From castle to manor I go.
I entertain ladies and lords and their guests. Always, I put on a good show.

They all like to hear stories of knights and chivalrous ways.
Tales of battlefield glories brighten my listeners' days.

Traveling Minstrel

Mary Wheeler

Fine (after 3rd verse)

(Minstrel exits. Narrator enters.)

Narrator: *(reads)*

The tournaments provided a show where knights were trained.
Magnificent occasions—noble families entertained.
Everyone liked village fairs.
Merchants came and sold their wares
In the middle of the Middle Ages.

A pyramid of power—the king was at the top.
Below him came the vassals, knights, and serfs who farmed the crops.
As the strong protected weak,
Feudalism reached its peak
In the middle of the Middle Ages.

(Sing *Illuminations*)

Illuminations

Illuminations are decorations on the pages of the books of yesterday.
Illuminations—Learn information.
Let us see how others used to work and play.

Illuminations

Mary Wheeler

Il-lu-mi-na-tions are dec-or-a-tions on the pa-ges of the books of yes-ter-day.

Il-lu-mi-na-tions - Learn in-for-ma-tion let us learn how oth-ers used to work and play.

1. A law and order government-they organized it well.
Their principles lived on although the Roman Empire fell.
Years of devastating wars
Passed as towns grew on the shores
In the middle of the Middle Ages.

2. A Conqueror named William, 1066 was crowned.
His ruthlessnesss and courage throughout Europe were renowned.
Into England, Normans came;
Lots of land the Duke would claim
In the middle of the Middle Ages.

3. 1095's when Christians began the First Crusade.
A journey to Jerusalem to win it back was made.
Eight Crusades, two hundred years -
Even children volunteered
In the middle of the Middle Ages.

4. His loyalty and service was promised to a lord.
The knight, a mighty warrior, could fight with lance and sword.
First, a page and then a squire,
Chain mail was his safe attire
In the middle of the Middle Ages.

5. The tournaments provided a show where knights were trained.
Magnificent occasions - noble families entertained.
Everyone liked village fairs.
Merchants came and sold their wares
In the middle of the Middle Ages.

6. A pyramid of power - the king was at the top.
Below him came the vassals, knights, and serfs who farmed the crops.
As the strong protected weak,
Feudalism reached its peak
In the middle of the Middle Ages.

7. King John had opposition; he went to Runnymeade.
He signed the Magna Carta, but reluctantly agreed.
1215 was when they met.
Liberties were what they'd get
In the middle of the Middle Ages.

8. A Lionhearted Richard and Henrys one, two, three
Were all among the heirs who served as English royalty.
With education on the rise
Tall cathedrals touched the sky
In the middle of the Middle Ages.

From In the Middle of the Middle Ages: Integrating Content Standards and the Arts. By Mary Wheeler and Jill Terlep. Music by Mary Wheeler. Illustrations by Jill Terlep. Westport, CT: Libraries Unlimited/Teacher Ideas Press. Copyright © 2007.

*(Spotlight **off**. Narrator exits. Children and Herald walk to center.)*

Act 3: Crusader, Horse, and King Arthur's Court

Scene 1

*(Spotlight **on center stage.** Crusader and horse are on stage.)*

Child 4: Oh, look, another knight, how exciting.

Child 1: That knight is going to the Crusades. He's not just any knight. He's one of the Knights of St. John. See his black surcoat with a white cross? A surcoat is a tunic worn over armor, you know.

Crusader: That is right. My order is usually called the Knights Hospitaller. We provide armed protection for the pilgrims. My brothers also care for the sick.

Herald: I've seen knights with white surcoats and red crosses. Who are they?

Crusader: They are the Knights Templar, another military order. In some Crusades, we protect the troops together.

Horse: I'm glad I only have one knight on my back. Some of my friends, horses with the Knights Templar, have to carry **two** knights because of their vow of poverty. With the armor, the weapons, the knights, and supplies… Whew! When he's wearing armor, that's an extra 40 or 50 pounds. Two knights would be a heavy load to carry. *(kneels down like he has a heavy weight on his back)*

Herald: I wish dragons got to go along with the knights into battle. That would be exciting.

(Crusader looks suspiciously at Herald.)

Child 2: Doesn't your armor consist of a helmet, shield, and a coat of chain mail?

Crusader: Yes, it does. We wear linen or leather underneath.

Horse: His armor is great, but I am his most important instrument for warfare. *(nodding importantly)* He learned to ride and care for me when he was a little boy. He fights his battles from my back using lances and swords.

Child 3: Who goes on the Crusades?

Crusader: In the First Crusade about thirty thousand people, from all walks of life, set out to recapture the Holy Land in 1096.

Child 1: I know about this. Pope Urban II appealed to the masses in 1095 and called for the freeing of Jerusalem for Christianity. Following Muhammad's death, the Turks gained power of the city. The First Crusade gained control of the city.

Crusader: The Second Crusade tried to regain control of the city after it was lost, again, after the First Crusade. And, so it continues with more and more Crusades, which is where we're headed now.

*(Sing **Marching to the Crusades**)*

Marching to the Crusades

Following Muhammad's death, a Holy War was waged.
Muslims ruled Jerusalem, and Christians were enraged.

From petty knights to local lords,
Some thousands heard the papal call.
The masses marched in the First Crusade,
'Twas barons, peasants, one and all.

To face their sins and save their souls –
"God wills it!" was their battle cry.
Crusaders marched to the Holy Land
Reclaiming power from days gone by.

(Horse and Knight)
Marching to the Crusades—together we're marching along.
Marching to the Crusades—together we're singing a song.

(Horse) I'm the horse,
(Knight) And I'm the knight.
(Horse) I can prance,
(Knight) And I can fight.

(Horse and Knight)
Marching to the Crusades—together we're marching along.

(Knight) I tried on my new metal armor.
I hoped to impress a young maid,
But my horse fell down when I got on his back.
(Horse)
He didn't warn me how much armor weighed.

(Horse and Knight)
Marching to the Crusades—together we're marching along.
Marching to the Crusades—together we're singing a song.

(Horse) I'm the horse,
(Knight) And I'm the knight.
(Horse) I can prance,
(Knight) And I can fight.

(Horse and Knight)
Marching to the Crusades—together we're marching along.

Marching to the Crusades

Mary Wheeler

From *In the Middle of the Middle Ages: Integrating Content Standards and the Arts*. By Mary Wheeler and Jill Terlep. Music by Mary Wheeler. Illustrations by Jill Terlep. Westport, CT: Libraries Unlimited/Teacher Ideas Press. Copyright © 2007.

Child 4: I really want to be a knight. The armor looks very important.

Horse: Don't forget the horse. The horse is VERY important.

Child 3: Oh, one more thing. We need to solve this riddle to help our friend, Harold. "Take a trip and you will learn. Hungry Herald should return after symbols; it's okay. Rumble, grumble goes away." Can you help?

Horse: I'd like to be a good NEIGH-bor—get it?—NEIGH-bor. But I don't know the answer.

Child 2: Well, thanks for telling us about the Crusades, Sir.

Crusader: You're welcome. We must be on our way. Good day.

(Horse and Crusader exit.)

Herald: *(Children hold Herald back.)* I guess I should just be glad that he didn't try to slay me. I didn't know we'd see so many knights on the road.

Child 1: Look, there are more people coming our way. Maybe they'll know where to get bread.

(King Arthur, Guinevere, and Merlin enter.)

King Arthur: How do you do, children? I am King Arthur.

Merlin: *(with flare and importance)* He's famous, you know. King Arthur and the Knights of the Round Table.

Child 4: More knights! That's great. I want to be a knight. We've met two today, already. Are the round knights traveling with you? *(looking around)*

Merlin: No, my child, they aren't "round" knights. They are the Knights of the Round Table.

Child 3: *(looking confused)* I don't see a round table. How do you travel with it?

Guinevere: Geoffrey of Monmouth wrote a book called *History of the Kings of Britain,* and in it he told the tales of King Arthur and his Round Table. That's us. How much of his stories was based on fact and how much on fiction is unknown, but everybody wants to read them.

Child 2: So, you may only exist in books, not in real life.

Merlin: Seems to be a lot of that going around today. *(looking very pointedly at Herald then back at the children)*

King Arthur: It is most likely that I am a famous warrior, or my character may have been based on more than one person, maybe a number of kings. Stories of my deeds have been told for hundreds of years.

Guinevere: The tales of King Arthur and his knights in shining armor are associated with love, bravery, chivalry, and maybe a belief in magic. We believe in those values and ideals.

King Arthur: Some stories say that I have a round table for my knights so that they won't fight for the important seat at the head of the table. At a round table, they're all equal. Only the bravest, most honorable knights are allowed at the table.

(Herald walks around Guinevere and steps on her veil.)

From *In the Middle of the Middle Ages: Integrating Content Standards and the Arts.* By Mary Wheeler and Jill Terlep. Music by Mary Wheeler. Illustrations by Jill Terlep. Westport, CT: Libraries Unlimited/Teacher Ideas Press. Copyright © 2007.

Guinevere: Excuse me, you're stepping on my veil.

Herald: I thought you might have some bread in there. It's very large.

Guinevere: I'm sorry. I have no bread for you. Please don't breathe fire on me.

Herald: I don't breathe fire. Like you, I'm a mythical creature from the Middle Ages. Besides, I'm not that scary. I'm a very small dragon. In books and stories, most dragons are bigger than elephants. That would even scare me *(shaking)*.

Merlin: Even imaginary or mythical creatures can be a little scary.

Child 2: *(looking at Merlin)* Who are you, Sir?

Merlin: I am Merlin. I am one of the most interesting figures in Arthurian stories. Geoffrey of Monmouth created me for his book about King Arthur. I'm also known as Merlinus. Depending on the story, I am Arthur's advisor, his magician in the court of Camelot, his prophet, and more. I have a very exciting life.

Child 1: This is a lot to take in today … mythical dragons, kings, queens, and magicians. It makes life at the castle seem pretty dull.

Merlin: Whether we are fact or fiction, all of the Arthurian figures—King Arthur, Guinevere, Sir Lancelot, and many others, as well as Excalibur and Camelot, and yours truly *(pointing to self with a flourish)*—fascinate and entertain.

Herald: Don't forget the dragons.

(Dancers enter.)

*(Sing **Castle in Motion**)*

Castle in Motion

(Guinevere)
Merlin the magician lived in the days of knights
And kings and queens and dragons who were very frightful sights.
Chivalry was Merlin's code, but magic was his trade.
In castles of medieval times, his wondrous tricks were played.

King Arthur summoned Merlin one dark and stormy night.
Said,

(King Arthur)
"Royal feasting's made me fat. My armor's much too tight."

(Guinevere)
So Merlin picked some palace chores to play some music to.
He created Castle-Motions for King Arthur's Court to do.

(Merlin)
Swim a moat. Row a boat.
Round the table if you're able.
Climb the tower. You've got the power.
Ride a horse, again, of course.
Stretch your bow. Knead the dough.
Shoot an arrow, straight and narrow.
Push a plow. You know how.
Stir the brew, backwards, too.
Foe on ridge, draw the bridge.
Scale a wall. Do not fall.
Catch the dragon. Load the wagon.
Wave your sword like a lord.

(All or Merlin)
Camelot was long ago. If Merlin lived today,
He would tell you,
"Listen close,"
And you would hear him say,
"Do the Castle-Motions to keep healthy and stay well.
Exercise is magic. You don't need a wizard's spell."

Do the Castle-Motions.

Castle in Motion

Mary Wheeler

From *In the Middle of the Middle Ages: Integrating Content Standards and the Arts.* By Mary Wheeler and Jill Terlep. Music by Mary Wheeler. Illustrations by Jill Terlep. Westport, CT: Libraries Unlimited/Teacher Ideas Press. Copyright © 2007.

(Dancers exit.)

Merlin: Oh, I love exercise. Castle life keeps us fit and healthy.

Child 1: A lot of things happen in our castle. It's a busy place.

Child 3: And a safe place.

Child 2: I like to climb the tower and look down at the countryside. From our position at the top of the hill, we can see for miles. That helps us prepare for attacks.

Child 3: The walls of the castle are several yards thick and built of stone. That keeps us safe, too.

Child 4: I love the moat and the drawbridge. We pull up the drawbridge so that our enemies can't come into the bailey, which is our courtyard. There are arrow loops in the walls. We can shoot arrows at anyone attacking us.

King Arthur: It sounds like you live in a very strong fortress. I have a strong fortress, too. Many say that my castle is in my realm of Camelot.

Merlin: Ah, Camelot. It's time to head home and do some more Castle Motions.

Guinevere: Yes, it is time. Good luck finding bread for your dragon. We're sorry that we could not help.

(Guinivere, King Arthur, and Merlin exit.)

Child 3: This has been a strange day.

Child 1: Let's continue to the village. I don't want to be outside the castle walls after dark. I'll get into trouble.

Child 2: Herald, we'll keep trying. We'll find some bread.

Herald: *(sadly)* I wish I knew how to get more bread. Maybe Merlin's magic would help.

(Spotlight off. Characters exit.)

Scene 2

*(Spotlight **on stage right**. Minstrel is on stage.)*

(Sing ***Traveling Minstrel***, chorus and third verse)

Traveling Minstrel

A traveling minstrel, my job is to sing. From castle to manor I go.
I entertain ladies and lords and their guests. Always, I put on a good show.

Show respect to the ladies. Prove your honor is true.
Bravely fight for your manor; that's what noblemen do.

Traveling Minstrel

Mary Wheeler

Fine (after 3rd verse)

From *In the Middle of the Middle Ages: Integrating Content Standards and the Arts.* By Mary Wheeler and Jill Terlep. Music by Mary Wheeler. Illustrations by Jill Terlep. Westport, CT: Libraries Unlimited/Teacher Ideas Press. Copyright © 2007.

(Minstrel exits. Narrator enters.)

Narrator: *(reads)*

> King John had opposition; he went to Runnymeade.
> He signed the Magna Carta, but reluctantly agreed.
> Twelve fifteen was when they met.
> Liberties were what they'd get
> In the middle of the Middle Ages.
>
> A Lion-Hearted Richard and Henrys one, two, three
> Were all among the heirs who served as English royalty.
> With education on the rise,
> Tall cathedrals touched the skies
> In the middle of the Middle Ages.

*(Sing **Illuminations**)*

Illuminations

> Illuminations are decorations on the pages of the books of yesterday.
> Illuminations—Learn information.
> Let us see how others used to work and play.

Illuminations

Mary Wheeler

1. A law and order government-they organized it well.
Their principles lived on although the Roman Empire fell.
Years of devastating wars
Passed as towns grew on the shores
In the middle of the Middle Ages.

2. A Conqueror named William, 1066 was crowned.
His ruthlessnesss and courage throughout Europe were renowned.
Into England, Normans came;
Lots of land the Duke would claim
In the middle of the Middle Ages.

3. 1095's when Christians began the First Crusade.
A journey to Jerusalem to win it back was made.
Eight Crusades, two hundred years -
Even children volunteered
In the middle of the Middle Ages.

4. His loyalty and service was promised to a lord.
The knight, a mighty warrior, could fight with lance and sword.
First, a page and then a squire,
Chain mail was his safe attire
In the middle of the Middle Ages.

5. The tournaments provided a show where knights were trained.
Magnificent occasions - noble families entertained.
Everyone liked village fairs.
Merchants came and sold their wares
In the middle of the Middle Ages.

6. A pyramid of power - the king was at the top.
Below him came the vassals, knights, and serfs who farmed the crops.
As the strong protected weak,
Feudalism reached its peak
In the middle of the Middle Ages.

7. King John had opposition; he went to Runnymeade.
He signed the Magna Carta, but reluctantly agreed.
1215 was when they met.
Liberties were what they'd get
In the middle of the Middle Ages.

8. A Lionhearted Richard and Henrys one, two, three
Were all among the heirs who served as English royalty.
With education on the rise
Tall cathedrals touched the sky
In the middle of the Middle Ages.

From *In the Middle of the Middle Ages: Integrating Content Standards and the Arts*. By Mary Wheeler and Jill Terlep. Music by Mary Wheeler. Illustrations by Jill Terlep. Westport, CT: Libraries Unlimited/Teacher Ideas Press. Copyright © 2007.

*(Spotlight **off**. Narrator exits. Children and Herald walk to center.)*

Act 4: Bride and Leo

(Spotlight on center stage.)

Child 1: This day has been interesting.

Child 2: And, exhausting. *(yawning)*

Child 3: But we still haven't solved the riddle that will get more bread for Herald.

Herald: I can't even think about the riddle with the rumble in my tummy.

Child 4: Let's read the clue, again.

Child 3: *(reads Clue from Minstrel)*
> Take a trip so you can learn.
> Hungry Herald should return
> After symbols; it's okay.
> Rumble, grumble goes away.

(Sing, ***This Riddle***)

This Riddle

This riddle is confusing,
And my brain I know I'm using,
But I need to solve this riddle right away.
This riddle's not amusing,
And it's minutes we are losing
'Cause poor Herald needs some food and yet today!

I'm thinking! I'm thinking! I'll get it I know.
To help Hungry Herald I'll search high and low.
I'm sure I will figure the answer, although
This riddle's not easy to solve, so, let's go!

This Riddle

Mary Wheeler

From *In the Middle of the Middle Ages: Integrating Content Standards and the Arts.* By Mary Wheeler and Jill Terlep. Music by Mary Wheeler. Illustrations by Jill Terlep. Westport, CT: Libraries Unlimited/Teacher Ideas Press. Copyright © 2007.

Child 2: It's confusing. I love riddles, but this one makes no sense. Why did he say "after symbols"? Do you think we'll find symbols along the road?

(Enter bride.)

Child 3: Hello, are you on your way to the village?

Bride: No, I am getting ready for my upcoming wedding.

Child 1: Where is your groom?

Bride: He lives on the other side of the village. Our families decided it would be a good marriage. The betrothal took place this year. If I were from a noble family, I would have been betrothed at age four or five years old. The groom's family would have chosen me for the power, money, and land that I brought to his family. Since I'm from the village, my family waited until they had the means to give me a good dowry to secure the engagement.

Child 2: What is a dowry?

Child 3: It's a gift to the groom. If you're a noble family, it might be a fief, that's land, and money, or other things you own. If you're from a peasant family, it could be a piece of furniture. Some villagers might offer a portion of land or even livestock.

Bride: That's what my family included in the dowry. *(Pointing to her cows)*

(Sing Two Cows)

Two Cows

I have one hundred sheep, and a boar, seven sows,
And three big draught horses to pull my two plows.
I bring to this marriage the rent from my land
Of forty-two shillings, along with my hand.
The dowry's been offered, and I am a ward.
My husband and the wedding were arranged by the lord.

I own two cows. I guess they go, too.
Will I be happy? I wish they knew.
I own two cows. I guess they go, too.
Will I be happy? I wish they knew.

I wish I knew.

Two Cows

Mary Wheeler

Herald: *(sadly, with great emphasis on first words)* **I wish I knew** how to get more bread.

Child 3: I wish we knew, too, Herald.

Child 4: *(focusing back on the bride)* As the bride, you bring a lot to the marriage. What does your groom bring?

Bride: I will receive one-third of my groom's estate as his dower.

Child 2: Are you headed to the church now?

Bride: No, the ceremony will be tomorrow. We'll have the marital ritual outside the church doors and follow with a mass inside the church. I must go now. I still have much to prepare for the wedding.

(Bride exits. Leonardo enters.)

Child 1: Hello. Are you heading to the village too, sir?

Leo: Yes, I am. My name is Leonardo Pisano, and I've arrived here from Italy. I'm going to teach the villagers how to use Arabic numerals.

Child 3: Why do the villagers need Arabic numerals, and what are they, Mr. Leo? Can I call you that?

Leo: Oh, sure. The cities have been growing so fast, and trade is increasing, too. We need better ways for accounting. We found out about the abacas during the tenth century, and it was a much faster way of figuring than "finger-reckoning." *(pauses and acts like he is counting on his fingers)* Roman numerals are still being used, but they aren't practical for solving arithmetic problems that need multiplication and division. We are ready for a change.

Child 2: Are these Arabic numerals the **change** that you speak of?

Leo: Yes. The symbols were developed in India around 400 B.C. by the Hindus. The Arabic people adopted them and spread them to other cultures. My father worked for the merchants of Pisa in North Africa, and he recognized the value of the Arabic numeral system. So do I. That's why I'm spreading the word.

Herald: Can you "spread the word" to us first? We're trying to solve a riddle.

Leo: *(holding up cards)* These are the Arabic figures: 1, 2, 3, 4, 5, 6, 7, 8, 9 and the sign 0.

Child 4: That's really interesting, Mr. Leo, but right now we have a problem. I think we need some magic to help poor Herald get some more bread. He just can't figure out how to get enough loaves of bread for him to eat each day. He always runs out.

Leo: *(excitedly)* That's it! That's it! You don't need magic. You need to be able to **calculate** the number of loaves of bread. Use those figures—1, 2, 3, 4, 5, 6, 7, 8, 9, and the sign 0—and you will always know how many will fill that tummy of yours, Herald.

Child 1: Mr. Leo, what do you mean, calculate?

Leo: Do it this way, Herald. Eat until you are full. Then, multiply the number of loaves by seven, that's for each day of the week. Here, I'll show you how to do it. *(pretends to figure on his scrolled paper, and Herald nods)* Then you can tell the cooks how many loaves to bake for you.

Child 1: But, what about the minstrel's clue?

Child 2: Let's think about the riddle. "Take a trip so you can learn." Wait! We walked around the countryside and **learned** about Crusades, pillories, peasants, horses, and even numerals!

Child 3: The clue says next, "Hungry Herald should return after symbols." Leo's number **symbols**! Leo's number symbols! 1, 2, 3, 4, 5, 6, 7, 8, 9 ...!

Child 4: The next words were, "It's okay. Rumble, grumble goes away." We solved the riddle! It's okay for Herald to go back to the castle and multiply for the number of loaves of bread he needs. His rumble, grumble stomach will be satisfied.

Everyone: Yeah! Thanks, Leo! *(dancing)*

Herald: We don't need magic. We just need Arabic numerals. Thanks, Leo. Thanks! I'm heading back to the castle right now. *(runs offstage)*

*(Spotlight **off**. All cast members and choir, if possible, wearing white gloves, enter stage for **Finale**. Optional— characters can join the choir if it's easier. Two people carry a treasure chest and place it up front and in the center. Herald quickly and secretly hides behind it, or in it.)*

FINALE

*(Spotlights **and all other lights are off**. Only **Black lights shine on choir and characters**. Everyone does hand motions to the music.)*

*(Sing **Magic or Me?**)*

Magic or Me?

Is it magic or is it me?
Imagination's the key.
It opens up a treasure chest,
And inside—the magic is me.

We searched the Middle Ages,
Saw a castle come alive.
Its story seemed to magically unfold.
A dragon started moving.
It was right before our eyes.
The drama was enchanting to behold.

Is it magic or is it me?
Imagination's the key.
It opens up a treasure chest,
And inside—the magic is me.

I am the magic.
I am the magic.
I am the magic.
I am the magic.

(All lights go on.)

(Herald pops out of the treasure chest.)

Surprise!
The magic is me.

(Children hold up scroll signs: "THE END" and "CHEER.")

Magic or Me?

Mary Wheeler

Audition Organization and Evaluation

Before holding auditions, tell the students about the *In the Middle of the Middle Ages* production that they are about to undertake. Build up enthusiasm ahead of time by describing the characters and relating the story. Announce the titles of the songs, and let them discover that they are going to be learning about the Middle Ages in a very unique and exciting way. Explain to the classes that the finished product is going to take a lot of work, but they are going to be creating memories for themselves and their friends for a lifetime!

Tips for the director:

- Give the students a choice and have them write it a few days before the auditions. Use the ***Lights! Camera! Action!*** letter (p. 186) to the students to give details on the audition process, the passage they will be reading, and the song that they will be singing, if applicable. The audition letter gives them the following choices:

What would you like to do in the program?

_____ Be a main character (a lot of memorizing)—Herald and the Palace Children

_____ Be a supporting character (less memorizing)—Peasant, Wife, Sir Richard, Crusader, King Arthur, Guinevere, etc.

_____ Appear on stage, but say only one line or two lines—extra peasants

_____ Be a dancer

_____ Sing in the choir

_____ Work in the stage crew

_____ Anything else you want to say? _____

- Consider having two sets of main characters, for the Introduction, Acts 1 and 2 and for Acts 3 and 4.
- Enlist adult help in casting.
- Give the first two pages of the play to everyone who wants to try out a couple of days ahead of time. Let them know that even though they are reading the part of Hungry Herald, for example, that is not necessarily the part for which they will be chosen.
- Conduct the auditions in front of an audience, including other children.
- Rate the students as they try out.
- Make sure the students who get singing parts can carry a tune!
- Try to match the students' abilities with the parts they chose.

Audition Evaluation Form

Page____ of ____

Student Name_____

Rate from 1 to 5, with a 5 being great.

Timing	Expression	Enthusiasm	Ability	Voice Control	Overall

Comments:_____
_____
_____

- -

Student Name_____

Rate from 1 to 5, with a 5 being great.

Timing	Expression	Enthusiasm	Ability	Voice Control	Overall

Comments:_____
_____
_____

- -

Student Name_____

Rate from 1 to 5, with a 5 being great.

Timing	Expression	Enthusiasm	Ability	Voice Control	Overall

Comments:_____
_____
_____

Lights! Camera! Action!

Our class is getting ready to stage a production of **In the Middle of the Middle Ages.**
Staging a play is a lot of work and a lot of fun.
On _____, we will hold auditions and select the production crew.

It is time to start thinking about how you would like to be involved.

For the auditions, students read a passage from the play. Those auditioning for singing roles will sing a short song. We will watch for qualities like enthusiasm, expression, and timing.

Good luck! We know that everyone will play a special part in this production.

Play Synopsis

Hungry Herald is a dragon who is befriended by the castle children. They must solve a riddle to help feed poor Herald who loves bread but never has enough. Traveling through the countryside, Herald and the children learn about life in the Middle Ages from interesting characters such as the minstrel, Crusader and his horse, peasant, and members of King Arthur's Court. Leonardo Pisano, an Italian mathematician, who introduces everyone to Arabic numerals and counting, provides the riddle's solution.

Song List

Salted Meats and Pickled Beets
Illuminations
Sir Richard
Marching to the Crusades
This Riddle

Traveling Minstrel
Sun Up, Sun Down
Pillory on the Village Green
Castle in Motion
Two Cows

Name _____

What would you like to do?

_____ Be a main character (a lot of memorizing)—Hungry Herald and Palace Children

_____ Be a supporting character (less memorizing)—Peasant, Wife, Crusader, etc.

_____ Appear on stage but only say one or two lines—extra peasants, etc.

_____ Be a dancer

_____ Sing in the choir

_____ Work with the stage crew—lighting, prop management, directing, etc.

Other ideas or comments: _____

_____

_____

_____

Cast

Narrator	
Hungry Herald	
Child 1	
Child 2	
Child 3	
Child 4	
Minstrel	
Peasant	
Peasant's Wife	
Sir Richard	
Pillory Man	
Crusader	
Horse	
King Arthur	
Guinevere	
Merlin	
Bride	
Leonardo	
Dancers	

Songs

Illuminations:

Traveling Minstrel:

Salted Meats and Pickled Beets:

Marching to the Crusades:

Sun Up, Sun Down (A Peasant's Life):

Sir Richard, Child to Knight:

Pillory on the Village Green:

Castle in Motion:

Two Cows:

This Riddle:

Magic or Me?:

Notes:

From *In the Middle of the Middle Ages: Integrating Content Standards and the Arts.* By Mary Wheeler and Jill Terlep. Music by Mary Wheeler. Illustrations by Jill Terlep. Westport, CT: Libraries Unlimited/Teacher Ideas Press. Copyright © 2007.

Dear Parents,

Our group is about to begin work on an educational musical, *In the Middle of the Middle Ages*, that will be presented to the school and community. This program is unique because students and audiences will learn about the Middle Ages as the musical is being practiced and performed. Each song and each storyline are written to inform the cast and audience about life in medieval times. While the project will end with a theatrical performance, it will also expand into the classroom. Historical facts and concepts will be taught as the show is being rehearsed.

The class will have fun and learn as they perform the songs. The musical contains lyrics that have been carefully researched, and every word is intended to instruct as well as entertain. The students can look forward to performing the following songs:

- How does a meal of cooked peacock and roasted eel sound? In *Salted Meats and Pickled Beets,* appetites are whetted for some unusual foods.

- The *Traveling Minstrel* performs again just for the lords and ladies and families of today. Listen to those "tales of battlefield glories."

- Get ready for lots of action with *Castle in Motion.* Every stage and choir member does aerobic movements that match the activities of medieval times. So "swim the moat" and "scale the wall" to the exciting times.

- From *Sun Up, Sun Down,* join the peasant and his wife as they struggle in the fields of the castle's shadow.

- Parade along with the Crusader and his horse, of course. Armor weighs a lot, but that won't stop any good steed from *Marching to the Crusades.*

- *Illuminations*—let's light up minds with knowledge and celebrate the intricate, decorations on the pages of long ago.

- It was a crime he didn't mean, so pity the poor man in the *Pillory on the Village Green.* Don't tease him, though.

- Solve *This Riddle* and learn of Leonardo Pisano's number symbols. Everyone needs to count their blessings.

- Could *Two Cows* really know if the bride is happy? Maybe the rest of her dowry—a boar, seven sows, and three big draught horses—will tell more.

- Say Sir Richard's name along with him and be proud of it in *Sir Richard, Child to Knight.*

We believe this will be a tremendous opportunity for your child to learn medieval history and display his or her talents, and we hope you are as excited as we are with the educational musical. We'll try to keep you informed as we proceed, and we look forward to seeing you at our formal presentation.

Sincerely,

Permission is granted for my child to be videotaped during the performance of the educational musical, *In the Middle of the Middle Ages*.

Child's Name _____

Signature of Parent or Guardian _____

Date _____ *(Please send this form back to school with your child by _____.)*

- -

Permission is granted for my child to be videotaped during the performance of the educational musical, *In the Middle of the Middle Ages*.

Child's Name _____

Signature of Parent or Guardian _____

Date _____ *(Please send this form back to school with your child by _____.)*

- -

Permission is granted for my child to be videotaped during the performance of the educational musical, *In the Middle of the Middle Ages*.

Child's Name _____

Signature of Parent or Guardian _____

Date _____ *(Please send this form back to school with your child by _____.)*

- -

Permission is granted for my child to be videotaped during the performance of the educational musical, *In the Middle of the Middle Ages*.

Child's Name _____

Signature of Parent or Guardian _____

Date _____ *(Please send this form back to school with your child by _____.)*

Dear Parents,

Earlier, you received a letter from our group telling you that we were beginning to work on an educational musical, *In the Middle of the Middle Ages*. This experience is a tremendous opportunity for your child to learn about medieval history and display his or her talents. Producing a program of this magnitude is a big project, but it is also a fun one. Not only will your child learn a lot about this important period in history, but he or she will be creating memories to last a lifetime!

A lot of time and effort go into the production of such a show, and we will do our best to accomplish as much as we can. As we proceed with practices and during the performances, we may call on volunteers to help us attain our goals. If you would like to help and can provide some time, we would appreciate your completing this survey and returning the paper with your child.

Please check any blanks where you can and would like to volunteer.

_____ Making costumes

_____ Decorating scenery

_____ Helping groups or individuals practice performances

_____ Managing sound systems

_____ Showing spotlights

_____ Copying papers for scripts, worksheets, letters, etc.

_____ Monitoring written work

_____ Organizing papers, props, children, etc. for the performance

_____ Designing and making programs

_____ Planning an "It's a Wrap" Party

_____ Providing snacks for practices or the final party

_____ Cleaning up

_____ Directing or accompanying music practices

Please note any other skills, talents, or services that you could offer.

_____

_____

_____

_____

_____

Telephone _____

E-mail _____

Volunteer's Name _____

We appreciate your help! We will contact you, if we can use your services. Thank you.

Dear Staff,

On _____ our group will present a dress rehearsal of the musical program *In the Middle of the Middle Ages* to the school. You are cordially invited to bring your class. The presentation will start at _____.

In addition to presenting a musical, our group has been studying the Middle Ages in the classroom, and we would like to share some of the history with your students. To help other classes learn more, here is some information about the production.

Synopsis

Hungry Herald is a dragon who is befriended by the castle children. They must solve a riddle to help feed poor Herald who loves bread but never has enough. Traveling through the countryside, Herald and the children learn about life in the Middle Ages from interesting characters such as the minstrel, Crusader and his horse, peasant, and members of King Arthur's Court. Leonardo Pisano, an Italian mathematician, who introduces everyone to Arabic numerals and counting, provides the riddle's solution.

The dialogue, action, and songs come together to teach the audience about the Middle Ages, as we entertain them. This is what your students will learn:

Introduction

Following the collapse of the Roman Empire, people no longer relied on protection from the government. Towns began to grow along the shores of rivers and streams.

In 1066, William the Conqueror crossed the English Channel and claimed the land.

Illuminations were decorations on the pages of books of long ago.

Act 1: Hungry Herald and the Children

Scene 1:

Hungry Herald, the Dragon, appears before the palace children. They hear a loud rumble and are afraid at first, but soon they realize the sound is only Herald's stomach growling because he is hungry. In *Salted Meats and Pickled Beets,* Herald mentions a lot of the foods that he eats such as peacocks, salted butter, and hard cheese. But his very favorite is bread, and he never gets enough of it!

The traveling minstrel provides a clue for Herald's need for more bread, and the children and Herald set off across the countryside in search of the answer.

Scene 2: *Traveling Minstrel/Illuminations*

The *Traveling Minstrel* entertains the lords and ladies while they are feasting. He puts on a good show, and later they dance to his music.

Starting in the year 1095, the Crusades lasted more than 200 years. The goal of the Christians was to win back Jerusalem.

Act 2: Peasant, Sir Richard, and Pillory

Scene 1

We listen as the peasant and his wife tell of their difficult struggles in *Sun Up, Sun Down*. Working in the fields, they stay in the castle's shadow.

Sir Richard proudly says his name again and again. After studying hard, he is dubbed a trusted knight in a solemn feudal rite.

Pity the poor man who is confined to the *Pillory on the Village Green*. All those who pass by know that in the future, he will always be fair.

Scene 2: *Traveling Minstrel/Illuminations*

From castle to manor the *Traveling Minstrel* goes. Tales of battlefield glories are the subjects of his tunes.

Tournaments are magnificent occasions where merchants sell their wares. Everyone enjoys the village fairs. Feudalism reaches its peak with the king at the top or the pyramid of power.

Act 3: Crusader, Horse, and King Arthur's Court

Scene 1

Heading to the Holy Land, "God wills it!" is their battle cry. That armor weighs a lot, but the horse and knight are still *Marching to the Crusades* along with the masses.

Oh, no! King Arthur can't fit into his armor, and it's Merlin to the rescue. With the *Castle in Motion,* everyone tries to exercise into shape. So get ready for lots of action.

Scene 2: *Traveling Minstrel/Illuminations*

Be sure to show respect to the ladies, and prove your honor is true. It's the age of chivalry, and the *Traveling Minstrel* gives good advice.

The Magna Carta was signed in 1215, but King John reluctantly agreed. Richard the Lion-Hearted and Henrys I and II and III were all English royal heirs.

Act 4: Bride and Leo

Leonardo Pisano, the Italian mathematician, finally helps the children solve *This Riddle*. Hungry Herald learns about the Arabic numerals, 1–9 and the sign 0, and discovers that he can **count** the number of loaves that he needs!

Can *Two Cows* know if a bride is going to be happy? Well, they are part of her dowry in the arranged marriage.

Finale

Is it *Magic or Me?* With imagination, a treasure chest of stories are told.

The program will probably last about an hour, and we will do our best to educate and entertain!

Sincerely,

Prop Checklist

- ☐ Narrator's Scroll (with *Illuminations* poem)
- ☐ Illumination Poster
- ☐ Bread
- ☐ Pillory
- ☐ White Gloves
- ☐ Treasure Chest
- ☐ Sound Effects for Herald's Stomach and Clippity Clop
- ☐ Spade or Tools
- ☐ Shield
- ☐ Animals for Bride
- ☐ Number Cards and Scroll for Leo
- ☐ Scroll Signs "The End" and "Cheer"
- ☐ _____
- ☐ _____
- ☐ _____
- ☐ _____
- ☐ _____
- ☐ _____
- ☐ _____
- ☐ _____
- ☐ _____
- ☐ _____

Performance Checklist

☐ Door and Picture onstage

☐ Ticket Takers with Tickets and Money Box

☐ Sound Coordinator

☐ Lighting Person

☐ Videographer

☐ Tables and Chairs for Ticket Takers, Sound Coordinator, Spotlight Person

☐ Props Prepared and Backstage

☐ Program Passers with Programs

☐ Music/Intercom, Arriving and Leaving

☐ Piano or Keyboard in Place with Music

☐ Microphones and Extensions Set Up

☐ Timeline Displayed

☐ Backdrops and Related Items in Place

☐ Choir Chairs

☐ Audience Seating

☐ Spotlights

☐ Light for Piano

☐ Scripts for Director, Musician, Production Helpers, etc.

☐ Costumes

☐ Blacklights

☐ _____

☐ _____

☐ _____

☐ _____

☐ _____

☐ _____

☐ _____

From *In the Middle of the Middle Ages: Integrating Content Standards and the Arts.* By Mary Wheeler and Jill Terlep. Music by Mary Wheeler. Illustrations by Jill Terlep. Westport, CT: Libraries Unlimited/Teacher Ideas Press. Copyright © 2007.

Bibliography

Juvenile Books

Alexander, Jonathon J. G. *Medieval Illuminators and Their Methods of Work*. New Haven: Yale University Press, 1992.

Bingham, Jane. *Medieval World, Usborne World History*. London: Usborne Publishing, 1999.

Clements, Gillian. *An Illustrated History of the World, How We Got to Where We Are*. New York: Farrar, Straus & Giroux, 1991.

Corbishley, Mike. *The Middle Ages (Cultural Atlas for Young People)*, rev. ed. New York: Facts on File, 2003.

Dawson, Imogen. *Food & Feasts in the Middle Ages*. Parsippany, NJ: New Discovery Books, 1994.

Gee, Robyn. *Living in Castle Times*. London: Usborne Publishing, 1991.

Howarth, Sarah. *The Middle Ages*. New York: Penguin Books, 1993.

Macdonald, Fiona. *A Medieval Castle*. New York: Peter Bedrick Books, 1990.

Macdonald, Fiona. *A Medieval Cathedral*. New York: Peter Bedrick Books, 1991.

Macdonald, Fiona. *How Would You Survive in the Middle Ages?* New York: Franklin Watts, 1995.

Macdonald, Fiona. *Women in Medieval Times*. Lincolnwood, IL: Peter Bedrick Books, 2000.

Adult Books

Barter, James. *Life in a Medieval Village*. San Diego, CA: Lucent Books, 2003.

Black, Professor Jeremy (general editor). *World History*. Bath, England: Parragon, 1999.

Blackwood, Gary L. *Life in a Medieval Castle*. San Diego, CA: Lucent Books, 2000.

Corzine, Phyllis. *World History Series—The Black Death*. San Diego, CA: Lucent Books, 1997.

Dance, Music, Theatre, Visual Arts: What Every Young American Should Know and Be Able to Do in the Arts: Developed by the Consortium of National Arts Education Associations. Reston, VA: Music Educators National Conference.

Fines, John. *Who's Who in the Middle Ages*. New York: Stein and Day, 1970.

Gies, Frances, and Gies, Joseph. *Marriage and the Family in the Middle Ages*. New York: Harper & Row, Publishers, 1987.

Gies, Frances, and Gies, Joseph. *Women in the Middle Ages*. New York: HarperPerennial, 1978.

Harpur, James. *Inside the Medieval World, A Panorama of Life in the Middle Ages.* London: Cassell Wellington House, 1995.

Lewis, Brenda Ralph, ed. *Great Civilizations.* Bath, England: Parragon, 1999.

Matthews, John (collected and retold by). *The Book of Arthur.* Old Saybrook, CT: Konecky & Konecky, 2002.

Merriam-Webster's School Dictionary. Springfield, MA: Merriam-Webster, 1999.

National Standards for History, Basic Edition. Los Angeles: National Center for History in the Schools, University of California, 1996.

Rice, Earle Jr. *Life During the Middle Ages.* San Diego, CA: Lucent Books, 1998.

Standards for the English Language Arts: A Project of National Council of Teachers of English & International Reading Association. Newark, DE: International Reading Association; Urbana, IL: National Council of Teachers of English, 1996.

Watson, Percy. *Building the Medieval Cathedrals.* Minneapolis, MN: Lerner, 1979 (original copyright 1976).

What Life Was Like in the Age of Chivalry. Editors of Time-Life Books. Alexandria, VA: Time-Life Books, 1997.

Additional Reading List

Avi. *The Book Without Words: A Fable of Medieval Magic.* New York: Hyperion Books for Children, 2005.

Adams, Simon. *Castles & Forts.* Boston: Kingfisher, a Houghton Mifflin Company Imprint, 2003.

Biesty, Stephen. *Castle.* First American ed. London, New York: Dorling Kindersley. Boston: Houghton Mifflin, 1994.

Cole, Joanna. *Ms. Frizzle's Adventures: Medieval Castle.* New York: Scholastic, 2003.

Cushman, Karen. *The Midwife's Apprentice.* New York: Clarion Books, 1995.

Dawson, Imogen. *Clothes & Crafts in the Middle Ages.* Parsippany, NJ: Dillon Press, 1997.

DePaola, Tomie. *Francis: The Poor Man of Assisi.* New York: Holiday House, 1982.

Elliott, Lynne. *Clothing in the Middle Ages.* New York: Crabtree Publishing Co., 2004.

Galloway, Priscilla. *Archers, Alchemists, and 98 Other Medieval Jobs You Might Have Loved or Loathed.* Toronto, Ontario: Annick Press Ltd., 2003.

Green, Robert. *William the Conqueror.* New York: Franklin Watts, 1998.

Haddix, Margaret Peterson. *Just Ella.* New York: Simon & Schuster Books for Young Readers, 1999.

Hastings, Selina, reteller. *Sir Gawain and the Loathly Lady.* New York: Lothrop, Lee & Shepard Books, 1985.

Heinrichs, Ann. *The Printing Press* (Inventions That Shaped the World series). New York: Franklin Watts, 2005.

Hilliam, David. *Castles and Cathedrals: The Great Buildings of Medieval Times.* New York: Rosen Pub., 2004.

Hilliam, David. *Thomas Becket: English Saint and Martyr.* New York: Rosen, 2005.

Hilliam, Paul. *William the Conquerer: The First Norman King of England.* New York: Rosen, 2005.

Hodges, Margaret, adapted from Edmund Spenser's *Fairie Queene. Saint George and the Dragon: A Golden Legend.* Boston: Little Brown, 1984.

Hodges, Margaret, reteller. *The Kitchen Knight: A Tale of King Arthur.* New York: Holiday House, 1990.

Howarth, Sarah. *What do we know about the Middle Ages?* New York: Peter Bedrick Books, 1998.

Kennedy, Robert F., Jr. *Saint Francis of Assisi: A Life of Joy.* New York: Hyperion Books for Children, 2005.

Langley, Andrew. *Eyewitness Medieval Life,* rev.ed. New York: DK Publishing, Inc., 2004.

Levine, Gail Carson. *Ella Enchanted.* New York: HarperCollins, 1997.

Marston, Elsa. *Muhammed of Mecca: Prophet of Islam.* New York: Franklin Watts, 2001.

Macaulay, David. *Building the Book Cathedral.* Boston: Houghton Mifflin, 1999.

Macaulay, David. *Castle.* Boston: Houghton Mifflin, 1977.

Macaulay, David. *Cathedral: The Story of Its Construction.* Boston: Houghton Mifflin, 1973.

MacDonald, Fiona. *Knights, Castles, and Warfare in the Middle Ages.* Milwaukee, WI: World Almanac Library, 2006.

Murrell, Deborah. *The Best Book of Knights and Castles.* Boston: Kingfisher, A Houghton Mifflin Company Imprint, 2005.

Lace, William W. *The Medieval Cathedral.* San Diego, CA: Lucent Books, 2001.

Leone, Bruno, ed. *The Middle Ages,* History Firsthand Series. San Diego, CA: Greenhaven Press, 2002.

Osborne, Mary Pope. *Favorite Medieval Tales.* New York: Scholastic Press, 1998.

Rice, Earle, Jr. *Life During the Middle Ages,* Way People Live Series. San Diego: Lucent Books, 1998.

Ross, Stewart. *Art and Architecture,* Medieval Realms Series. San Diego: Lucent Books, 2004.

Ross, Stewart. *Monarchs* (Medieval Realms series). San Diego: Lucent Books, 2004.

Stanley, Diane. *Saladin: Noble Prince of Islam.* New York: HarperCollins, 2002.

Steele, Philip. *The World of Castles.* Boston: Kingfisher, a Houghton Mifflin Company imprint, 2005.

Steer, Dugald, ed. *Dr. Ernest Drake's Dragonology: The Complete Book of Dragons.* Cambridge, MA: Candlewick Press, 2003.

Walker, Jane. *100 Things You Should Know about Knights & Castles.* Broomall, PA: Mason Crest, 2003.

Weatherly, Myra. *William Marshall: Medieval England's Greatest Knight.* Greensboro, NC: Morgan Reynolds, 2001.

Wildsmith, Brian. *Saint Francis.* Grand Rapids, MI: Eerdmans, 1996.

Wilkes, Angela. *A Farm through Time.* New York: DK Children's, 2001.

Woolf, Alex. *Death and Disease,* Medieval Realms Series. San Diego, CA: Lucent Books, 2004.

About the Authors

Mary Wheeler has more than 35 years of teaching experience in the Indiana public schools. She received her B.S. in Education from Ball State University and her M.S. in Education from Indiana University. Mary has been awarded the *Lilly Endowment* grant for Teacher Creativity. She has addressed the delegation of Indiana Historical Society members, detailing the use of music and drama to teach Indiana history. She is a longstanding member of the National Education Association, Indiana State Teachers' Association, Parent Teacher Organization, and the Shelby Eastern Classroom Teachers' Association.

Mary has been writing and producing educational activities, music, and musicals since 1979. She lives in Noblesville, Indiana, with her husband, John. She likes to spend her free time writing music and playing with her grandchildren.

Jill Terlep graduated from Purdue University with a B.S. in Economics. She has been a successful territory manager for both Hormel Foods and Bristol-Myers Squibb. Jill was responsible for teaching advanced wound care to nurses and physicians, along with patient teaching and counseling, while working with Bristol-Myers Squibb's medical products division. Jill conducted regular continuing education classes and nursing in-services. "Teaching, no matter what the subject, challenges your creativity and provides the opportunity to positively impact people's lives," says Jill.

Currently, Jill lives in Naperville, Illinois, with her husband, Jeff, and children, Drew and Lauren.

Mary and Jill are also the authors of *13 Colonies! 13 Years! Integrating Content Standards and the Arts to Teach the American Revolution.*

www.ingramcontent.com/pod-product-compliance
Lightning Source LLC
Chambersburg PA
CBHW080745250426
43672CB00032B/2855